Includes DVD with layout
kits, fonts, and more!

PICTURE YOURSELF
Creating
Digital Scrapbooks

Step-by-Step Instruction for Preserving Memories
Using Your Computer

Lori J. Davis and Sally Beacham

ISBN-10: 1-59863-488-7

ISBN-13: 978-1-59863-488-4

Library of Congress Catalog Card Number: 2007938242

Printed in the United States of America

08 09 10 11 12 BU 10 9 8 7 6 5 4 3 2 1

Publisher and General Manager, Thomson Course Technology PTR:
Stacy L. Hiquet

Associate Director of Marketing:
Sarah O'Donnell

Manager of Editorial Services:
Heather Talbot

Marketing Manager:
Jordan Casey

Acquisitions Editor:
Megan Belanger

Project Editor:
Jenny Davidson

Technical Reviewer:
Angela Cable

PTR Editorial Services Coordinator:
Erin Johnson

Copy Editor:
Kim Benbow

Interior Layout:
Shawn Morningstar

Cover Designer:
Mike Tanamachi

DVD-ROM Producer:
Brandon Penticuff

Indexer:
Sharon Shock

Thomson Course Technology PTR,
a division of Thomson Learning Inc.
25 Thomson Place
Boston, MA 02210
http://www.courseptr.com

THOMSON

COURSE TECHNOLOGY

Professional ■ Technical ■ Reference

This book is dedicated to our "boys"—thanks for helping, supporting, fixing, doing, being, and loving!

LORI & Sally

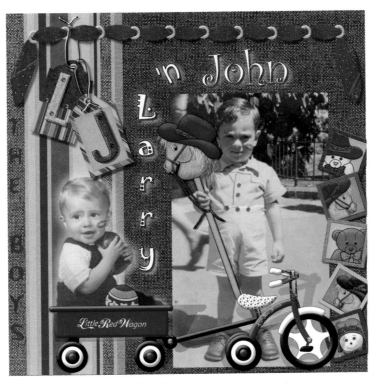

*Layout produced with scrapbook components by
Glenda Ketcham, on this book's resource DVD.*

Acknowledgments

WHERE DO WE BEGIN? So many people to thank, so little space! We need another book!

Let's start with the impetus behind this book—Megan Belanger at Course Technology PTR. We'll add in our editors Jenny Davidson (Lightning), Kim Benbow (Queen of the Commas), and Angela Cable (She Who Does It All). And a shout out to Brandon Penticuff (DVD Divine).

And then there's the unbelievably talented and generous group of designers who shared their work with us. Diverse in age, geography, and lifestyle, they are united by one common bond—the love of scrapbooking. Lauren Bavin, Angela Cable (see, we told you she did it all!), Doris Castle, Roberta D'Achille, Lie Fhung, Glenda Ketcham, and Terry Maruca—we thank you from the bottom of our hearts. We'd also like to extend those thanks to your Creative Team members who created beautiful scrapbook projects for this book from your designs.

We'd like to recognize our designers who provided additional cover art—Lauren Bavin, Doris Castle, Roberta D'Achille, Lie Fhung, Glenda Ketcham, Terry Maruca, Erica Nunez, and Ramona Vaughn. Thanks for creating beautiful layouts and for having unbelievably good-looking children, as well.

In addition, we'd like to thank Don Bozek at Strathmore Artist Papers, Amy Lemelin at Hawk Mountain Papers, Harald Heim at The Plugin Site, Kristina Foxworthy at Twisting Pixels, Doug Meisner and Nancy Peterson at Corel, Ben Hazard at Alien Skin, Alex Shalikashvili at AV Bros, Ray Larabie at Larabie Fonts, Kevin King at Kingthings, Howard Dickson at sheilsoft.com, Aaron Epstein at Color Schemer, Amy Edwards and her team at Scrapbook Bytes, Stacy Mann and her folks at Digital Scrapbook Pages, and all the gang at Digital Scrapbook Place, especially Lauren Bavin, head designer.

Very special thank yous go out to two of our dearest friends—Ron Lacey, whose friendship is only rivaled by his photographs, and the ever-creative Norene Malaney. Kris Zaklika and Janet Weinkranz deserve special mention, as well. Thanks, too, to Dimitry Belov, Mei Liu, Channen McGhee, Robin "Hoods" Rowlands, and the Knezevich clan.

Finally, we thank our families, for putting up and bearing with, coddling, cuddling, and cooking—especially the cooking! We also thank them for being, however unwillingly, our favorite models and scrapbook subjects. Larry, John, Peter, Ann, George, Nina, Dominic, Wade, Emilie, Brittanie, and our two favorite (little) boys—Anthony and Theodore, thank you all.

And of course we can't forget our feline family, Moussie, Edna, Little Max, Omar...for reminding us that life doesn't get any better than a full bowl of Meow Mix and a scratch behind the ears.

About the Authors

LORI J. DAVIS has authored and co-authored several books on Paint Shop Pro and digital scrapbooking. She has been teaching computer graphics classes online for about a dozen years, covering Adobe Photoshop Elements and Corel PHOTO-PAINT in addition to Paint Shop Pro. She has served as a beta tester for several graphics-related applications and has contributed a series of articles to *Digital Camera Magazine.* When she's not immersed in graphics, Lori enjoys photography, gardening, beading, knitting, and walking on the beach with her husband, Larry.

SALLY BEACHAM is the author of several books about Paint Shop Pro and digital scrapbooking. She teaches and writes material for www.lvsonline.com and has contributed numerous articles and other materials to major publications. She is currently employed as the "organizational technocrat" for a mid-size company in the hospitality industry in southern Maine. Sally and her husband John share seven children, two grandchildren, two cats, and very little free time. Her favorite color is pink, her favorite sport is cricket, her favorite food is not Brussels sprouts, and her favorite word is "Teddy."

Table of Contents

Introduction

SCRAPBOOKING, MEET COMPUTER. Computer, this is Scrapbooking.

Well, it's not quite that simple, but basically—it's that simple. Take the beloved craft (or art, as you see fit to term the concept) of scrapbooking and do it on your computer. Put away the mounds of supplies and the expensive tools, and use your dining room table for family meals once again. You can create beautiful scrapbook layouts and do so in the same style as you might construct traditional paper layouts, in less time, with no mess, no trips to the craft store, and significantly less expense.

Who This Book Is For

This book is written for the novice digital scrapbooker and the experienced paper scrapbooker who wants to dive into digital. It's also designed to be inspiration for the intermediate or experienced digital scrapbooker, who can peruse the layouts by our featured designers and their creative teams, and use the book's resource DVD contents in their own unique way.

This book is primarily written for use with PC computers running Windows, but rest assured that Mac devotees can scrapbook just as well. All the layout kits included on the resource DVD contain components that will work with both PC and Mac systems. Some of the utilities, plug-ins, and fonts may not, but an online search will turn up comparable items on the Internet.

The authors make these basic assumptions about the reader:

- You have access to a computer powerful enough to handle the software needed.

- You have a basic knowledge of your computer's operating system and features, can execute common application commands without additional instruction, and can install necessary software as needed without our assistance.

- You want to have fun, but promise to come up for air occasionally, once you're assimilated by the ScrapBorg!

"Mark and the Art of Motorcycle Maintenance" layout by Lori J. Davis. Components and papers from Lie Fhung's Ztampf Painting Kit, included on this book's resource DVD.

What You'll Find in This Book

In this book you'll learn about the history and traditions of scrapbooking, design and color theory, and the technical aspects and requirements of digital scrapbooking. And you'll get up to speed on some scrapbook terminology (so you can talk the lingo with all those other scrapbookers you'll discover!).

You'll also learn how to quickly assemble layouts or entire albums, how to correct and enhance your photographs so they'll be shown to their best advantage, and how to create your own scrapbook components. Finally, you'll have a book filled with inspiration that you can refer to when you need a jumpstart creating your own unique masterpieces.

We've left you some surprises sprinkled throughout the pages of this book. Each chapter begins with an image specially chosen to reflect the spirit of scrapbooking, the talent of our designers, and the content of the chapter. Most of these are designed from components that can be found on the resource DVD. Each chapter's text begins with a special "drop cap" initial P, which is made from components from our designers, and the very special alpha collection provided by Digital Scrapbook Pages, which can also be found on the book's DVD. In addition, our cover art images are layouts that can be found throughout the book. Please enjoy looking at these, and using them for inspiration, as much as we do.

"Brittanie" layout by Sally Beacham. Scrapbook components and font by Terry Maruca, Chris Beasley, and Tina Raparanta, all on this book's resource DVD.

How This Book Is Organized

This book consists of eleven chapters and one appendix. The chapters are divided into four sections: Part I, "Scrapbook Basics" (Chapters 1-4), Part II, "It's All About the Photos" (Chapters 5-8), Part III, "Adding to Your Toolbox" (Chapters 9 and 10), and Part IV, "Scrapbook Inspiration" (Chapter 11).

- **Chapter 1, Scrapbooking Why and How.** You'll begin by learning all about types of scrapbooks, tools needed to scrapbook, and costs associated with scrapbooking.

- **Chapter 2, DigiScrapping 101.** Here you'll find basic layout construction guidelines and "before you start" information.

- **Chapter 3, Creating Your First Layout.** See how to make great layouts from templates or scratch, using pre-made elements. Add text and photos to complete your page.

- **Chapter 4, Hybrid Scrapbooking.** Not only scrapbook pages but beautiful craft projects can be created using digital images. You'll see how here.

- **Chapter 5, Handling the Hardware.** In this chapter you'll take a look at what you need to know about some of the equipment you'll be using, including digital cameras, scanners, printers, and graphic tablets.

- **Chapter 6, Photo Editing Fundamentals.** Here you'll begin with the basics of editing photos, such as rotating and straightening, cropping and resizing, and color correction.

- **Chapter 7, Advanced Photo Techniques.** Delve into more advanced photo editing, including cropping techniques, manual adjustments of color and contrast, and converting color photos to black and white.

- **Chapter 8, Further Fun with Photos.** Editing photos isn't just a chore. There are lots of fun things you can do with your photos. In this chapter, you'll explore compositing, creating photo montages and panoramas, giving the subject of a portrait a digital face-lift, and converting photos into digital drawings and paintings.

- **Chapter 9, Creating Your Own Components.** Scrapbook kits are handy and fun to use, but why not create scrapping components of your own! We'll get you started with techniques for creating background papers, mats, frames, brads, eyelets, ribbons, and fibers. We'll also take a brief look at what you can do with brushes and how to create your own brushes.

- **Chapter 10, Enhancing Your Pages with Filters and Layer Styles.** Whether you're enhancing text, modifying existing scrapping components, or creating your own components, you'll want to make the most of filters and layer styles. In this chapter, you'll explore the types of filters and layer styles that are built into your image editor and how you can expand the capabilities of your image editor with plug-in filters.

Chapter 11, Inspiration. Here you'll find inspiration from layouts, techniques, and tips using the layout kits and resources found on the book's DVD. See how our featured designers and some of their Creative Team members use the kits to create unique pages and craft projects, and get ideas for your own pages.

Appendix A, Resources. One book is never enough. When you want more, explore the online resources outlined here!

What's on the DVD

We've gotten together such a large and varied assortment of resources for you that they couldn't all fit on a CD-ROM! This book includes a DVD, divided into five sections:

Kits and Components. Complete scrapbook kits and "alphabets" from several well-known and talented scrapbooking designers. (Located in the \Kits_and_ Elements folder.)

Fonts. Over 100 fonts from professional font designers, especially selected for you by Lori and Sally. (Located in the \Fonts folder.)

Plug-ins and Utilities. Freeware plug-in filters, as well as demos of other great filters, and some utilities that are handy for scrappers. (Located in the \Plugins_ and_Utilities folder.)

Tutorials. A few tutorials written for Paint Shop Pro Photo X2 and Photoshop Elements 6.0. If you use a different version of these image editors—or even a different one altogether—you might still get good ideas from these. (Located in the \Tutorials folder.)

Miscellany. A grab-bag of components, seamless tiles, fonts, and other miscellaneous goodies from Lori, Sally, and their buddy Robin "Hoods" Rowlands. (Located in the \Miscellany folder.)

There are two ways you can access the resource files on the DVD:

In your Web browser, load the index.html file located at the root directory of the DVD.

Browse the various folders of the DVD directly using your operating system's file navigator. (Windows users can use Windows Explorer.)

Be sure to read the terms of use for the different resources. And, most importantly, have fun!

"Lion" layout by Angela M. Cable.
Porcelain alpha by Angela, available at neocognition.com.

Part I
Scrapbook Basics

Scrapbook components by Roberta D'Achille and Angela Cable.

three girls

Emilie
Elliott
Sally
Briry

1990 and 1958

1

Scrapbooking Why and How

PICTURE YOURSELF IN THE wondrous world of digital scrapbooking. This is a world populated with computers, cameras, pixels, and printers—all devoted to helping you preserve memories in a style and format that suits your needs. We'll be your guides as you travel through the world of computer-generated memory page construction.

Why scrapbook? Because you can save all the family memories for your children and your children's children. Because scrapbooking is creative, relaxing, and rewarding. And—because scrapbooking is FUN.

How to scrapbook? That's what we're here for! Even if you've never been introduced to scrapbooking in any form, we can help you learn to use all the tools and find all the resources you need to get started. We'll teach you what you need to know to create beautiful digital scrapbook layouts. Before you finish this book, you'll be able to save your own memories as creatively as Figure 1.1 shows.

Figure 1.1

"Teddy and Roberta" digital scrapbook layout by Roberta D'Achille.

The Scrapbooking Concept

WHAT'S A SCRAPBOOK?
Why scrapbook? Who scrapbooks?
Why use a computer to help scrapbook?

All excellent questions—let's start with "What's a scrapbook?" For generations, people have documented life's experiences by saving memorabilia and photographs in albums for themselves and others to enjoy. Often these pages include decorative accents and text called *journaling* by scrapbookers. Traditionally, these pages, also known as *layouts*, are stored in albums of many sizes and types.

Scrapbooking is a very personal concept, and some consider it personal art. It's also flexible, and encompasses a multitude of techniques, both artistic and craft-oriented. Scrapbooking encourages even the most inexperienced photographer to create beautiful and meaningful arrangements and challenges the experienced designer to make some magic.

Some scrapbooks have themes, such as weddings or a new baby. Some scrapbooks document events, such as an entire scrapbook devoted to a cruise vacation. In Figure 1.2, notice the layout examples celebrating family, pets, travel, hobbies, and everyday (or sometimes not so everyday!) events. Heritage scrapbooks are popular. These are journals that record genealogical information and incorporate family pictures, sometimes with antique photos as well as period memorabilia.

Creating a scrapbook can be a relaxing hobby, an interesting avocation, and an important record of past and current history for future generations. Many scrapbookers enjoy meeting for communal events called *crops* (a reference to cropping photographs to fit the available layout space). Scrapbooking is popular in many countries, although supply sources may be somewhat limited. Sometimes the communal events involve using Web forums, e-mail lists, and chat applications.

Figure 1.2

Computer-generated scrapbook layouts by Lauren Bavin, Angela Cable, Doris Castle, Roberta D'Achille, Lie Fhung, Glenda Ketcham, and Terry Maruca.

It's become increasingly popular to use computers to assist in creating scrapbooks. The most common form of digital scrapbooking is creating text journaling and heading banners. The sheer variety of available fonts makes this task not only easy, but extremely flexible. However, today's scrapbooker can go as far as to create entire layouts from start to finish with a computer and various types of software. It's also easy to print the entire layout in one fell swoop, or save it to a CD-ROM for storage purposes or to share with others. Sometimes, layouts are shared via Web galleries, as shown in Figure 1.3, or personal Web sites as well.

Figure 1.3

Member Gallery at www.digitalscrapbookpages.com (courtesy of Glenda Ketcham).

Traditional Paper Scrapbooks

Paper scrapbook pages can be created in a variety of sizes and more styles than one can even imagine. Commonly, a scrapbook layout is placed in a plastic sleeve protector to help safeguard it from dust, dirt, and fingerprints (people *do* actually look at their scrapbooks). The sleeve protectors are stored in an album, oftentimes with a decorative cover. The paper layout in Figure 1.4 is designed as two 12 inch×12 inch cardstock-mounted layouts for facing pages in an album.

Figure 1.4

Traditional paper layout by Sally Beacham (photos by Ron Lacey).

Albums can be purchased in a variety of sizes. Often you'll find 12×12 inch and 8.5×11 inch (the dimensions of the paper layouts, not necessarily the external dimensions of the book itself). Other available sizes include 12×15 inch, 8×8 inch, 6×6 inch, and 5×7 inch. You can even create your own custom size using a binding machine.

The album binding itself is also a variable. The most popular binding types are *strap-hinge* (a metal strap goes through holes in the pages and the binding) and *post-bound* (expandable metal posts create the binding). Page protectors usually are *top-loading*—the layout is inserted from the top of the sleeve, making it more difficult for attachments to fall out of the protector if they become dislodged. You can also use three- or five-ring binders with pre-punched holes in the protectors. If you choose to create digital layouts and print them, you can still use the same types of albums and page protectors to showcase them. Figure 1.6 shows examples of post-bound and strap-hinge albums.

Figure 1.6

Post-bound and strap-hinge album bindings (courtesy of Amy Lemelin).

Figure 1.5

Calendar cards by Lie Fhung and Ztampf!.

Journals and Altered Books

There are a number of variations on the scrapbook concept. A couple of those are journals and altered books. A *journal* is a scrapbook that concentrates on the text aspect; it still incorporates photos and images, but generally tells a cohesive story from beginning to end. Journals are easy for the digital scrapper to create—all it takes is a word processor and some clip art.

Altered books are actual books that become the bound medium for collage-style scrapbooking. You can find them at second-hand stores, yard sales, and flea markets. Sometimes the book itself is an intrinsic part of the scrapbook theme, as shown in Figure 1.7. The altered book format can be an interesting way to display computer-generated scrapbook art.

Hybrid Scrapbooking

Combine digital techniques with paper scrapbooking resources and what do you get? Hybrid scrapbooking! You can design layouts and other paper crafts right on your computer, print them out, and then adhere or affix them to objects like calendars, recipe cards and books, blocks and other wooden items, decorative containers, jewelry, and even candles! (See Figure 1.8.)

Figure 1.8

Key tag, chipboard, and block albums by Lauren Bavin.

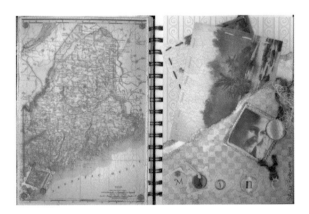

Figure 1.7

Altered journal by Sally Beacham.

Paper vs. Digital Scrapbooking

WHAT ARE THE ADVANTAGES of each type of scrapbooking? What do you need to start digital scrapbooking, what's it going to cost, and how does it compare to traditional paper scrapbooking?

Pros and Cons

Digital scrapbooking has a number of significant advantages over paper-based scrapbooking. The disadvantages make a short list, so let's start with those:

- Paper scrapbookers love the feel of handling components and the process of physically creating artwork with their hands and tools. That hands-on feel that is so satisfying when creating a layout such as the one seen in Figure 1.9 doesn't seem quite the same when you're cutting and pasting with a mouse.

- Digital scrapbooking doesn't require as many tools and accessories, but the tools you do need are major purchases—printers, scanners, and computers!

- If you have no background knowledge, it's not as fast and easy to learn how to produce an effect on a computer as it is to learn to cut a paper shape or layer paper for a layout.

Figure 1.9

Traditional 8×8 double-page paper layout by Sally Beacham. (Papers and embellishments by K & Company.)

On the other hand, the advantages of digital scrapbooking are countless. Here are just a few:

- Since many of us already own most of the hardware and a lot of the necessary software for digital scrapbooking, it can be a much less expensive way to document memories. Paper scrapbooking tools and supplies can be expensive, and you need a lot of them.

- Digital resources are infinitely reusable. Once you use a package of real eyelets, they're gone and you must buy more. One computer-generated image of an eyelet can be used over and over and modified in size and color to match any design scheme.

- Storage space! Finding storage space for all those paper scrapbooking supplies is a major undertaking—if you don't have a separate craft area or room, your family might find the dining room table overrun with scrapbook tools.

Digital scrappers keep all their supplies and works in progress on computer media storage, just like any other data file. The work area is confined to the computer area, which may already be an integral part of your home's design.

- Digital scrapbooking is flexible. Layouts can quickly be changed in size, design scheme, and color. Try doing that with paper.

- Once you're familiar with the software, you can work quickly. And, you can create multiple copies at the same time—so if you want to create a theme scrapbook for yourself, and other family members decide they want one too, you can print all of them together.

- Creating layouts digitally removes much of the necessity for maintaining strict archival-quality standards for photos. Since you're always working with a digital copy and not an original, another copy can be generated in seconds should something happen to the first one.

- Digital photos can be edited (usually in the same software you use to create the layout), saving time as well as allowing you to correct and enhance photos and even create special effects.

- Computer-generated layouts can be archived as data files to preserve copies or to print at a later date. They can be created as Web graphics for display on a Web site or gallery or burned to a CD for viewing. They can also be sent via e-mail to far-away friends and family.

Using a computer to enhance and create scrapbooking can be as simple or complex as you would like. Sometimes, you might just add computer-generated journaling and title banners to paper layouts to compensate for poor handwriting, or to make use of the thousands of terrific font types and styles, many of them free on the Internet. In Figure 1.10, the artist used text as an integral part of the layout design.

Figure 1.10

"15 Things" by Lauren Bavin.

Other ways you can add digital components to your scrapbooking is to create your own clip art to use as stickers, shapes, and realistic-looking embellishments, all without adding bulk to your pages.

Digital scrapbooking has a language and terminology all its own. The popular paper scrapbook term for decorative objects added to a paper layout is *embellishments*. Digital scrappers refer to computer-generated embellishments as *elements*. We'll use the term embellishment for both so as not to confuse "elements" with the software application Photoshop Elements, which will also be covered here in the book.

Figure 1.11

Baby album pages by Glenda Ketcham.

Sometimes, digital scrapbookers design page layouts that leave space for photos to be added after the layout is printed. This is useful if you're creating gift albums for someone else, and don't have the actual pictures that will be included. Perhaps a new baby is on its way, but not yet here. You can make an album of pre-constructed pages and present it as a shower gift before Baby even arrives. Figure 1.11 shows pre-made album pages and the finished result.

Of course, if you'd like to create a totally digital page, you can do that too, with the entire layout created on the computer, including the photos, which can be digitally corrected and enhanced, cropped, and sized to fit your page perfectly. Then the layout can be printed as is, stored for later printing, archived, resized for display in a Web gallery, or sent through e-mail. Once the layout is constructed, it's a simple matter to create many types of media from it.

What Does Scrapping Cost?

We've already mentioned that digital scrapbook resources are reusable—create or purchase a computer-generated embellishment and it's yours forever to modify as you like to use in as many layouts as you want.

Perhaps you wonder how much it will cost to create your own digital scrapbooks. The short answer is *a lot* less than paper scrapbooks of the same design and complexity. You probably already own a computer, but you might want to add some additional RAM, as scrapping with a paint program requires quite a bit of memory resources. (Anything over 1 gigabyte of RAM should be adequate, but the sky's the limit when it comes to memory—the more the merrier.)

There are two areas where you are likely to spend some money: software to produce your layouts and the method you use to print them. We'll discuss software later in this chapter and printers in Chapter 5, "Handing the Hardware," but let's devote a little time to printing methods right now.

If you don't want to print your layouts at home, other options include having them printed by a photo-finisher, in which case you'll want to design your layouts in a common photo print size, such as 8×10- inch. You can also have layouts printed by office supply and copy shops as a color photocopy. Generally, the largest size that can be economically printed is on 11×14-inch paper, which means using a standard paper size of 11×17 inches and trimming it. Then you can mount the layout on regular 12×12-inch cardstock sheets for placement in an album.

Smaller albums are available, which allow you to have layouts printed in 5×7- or 4×6-inch sizes. Layouts printed as snapshots and placed in a small album are convenient to display and very handy for smaller hands to use.

Of course, you don't have to print digital layouts at all. You can choose to store and view them as digital images, perhaps burned to CD-ROM or DVD for easy viewing, which is a cheap and portable way to store them. If you go this route, you might want to use a slide-show creator to present the layouts. Some of these applications can even incorporate music and sound files. If you are using Windows Media Center or Vista as an operating system (or Mac OS) you already have some tools and features that will let you create slide shows and DVDs without installing additional software.

Layouts can also be shown in Web galleries and on personal Web sites. Many of the digital scrapbook resource sites include picture galleries where members can display their scrapbook layouts:

- www.digitalscrapbookplace.com
- www.scrapbook-bytes.com
- www.pagesoftheheart.net
- www.digitalscrapbookpages.com
- www.twopeasinabucket.com
- www.renderedmemories.com (shown in Figure 1.12)
- www.scrapbookgraphics.com/galleries/

You'll find lots of resources for digital scrappers (as well as some paper scrapbook information) at these sites, from free downloadable digital components to chat forums for live interaction with other scrapbookers.

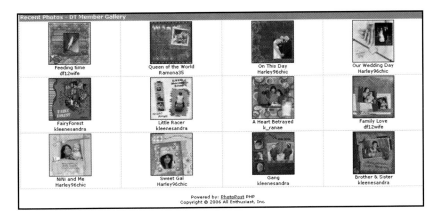

Figure 1.12

User Gallery at www.renderedmemories.com.

Digital Scrapbook Necessities and Niceties

ITEMS SUCH AS COMPUTERS and software are necessities for digital scrapbooking, but there are lots of other "nice-to-haves" that can make the digital scrapbook process easier, more fun, and more flexible.

Hardware and Peripherals

Computer hardware types abound, almost all of them useful for digital scrapbooking. It's not necessary to have or use all the types presented, but each peripheral adds another dimension to your ability to scrapbook.

Scanners

A scanner is handy to have, as most photos came into existence long before the days of consumer digital cameras. Scanning in old photos provides a nearly instantaneous means to archive precious and unique photos as well as multiple copies for many uses. You can have this done professionally, but it's fairly expensive and less convenient than scanning in your home at a moment's notice. (We'll examine consumer-level scanners further in Chapter 5.)

Printers

A printer is almost a must-have for a digital scrapbooker. Printers can be used to print photos, layout elements, or entire pages. If you want a mostly traditional paper layout, you can print journaling blocks and page titles only. It's possible to create your own text and photo transparency sheets.

Scrapbook Central!

Some local scrapbook stores have installed a scanner/printer combination from Epson called Scrapbook Central. This is a computer workstation with a scanner and printer, capable of scanning up to an 11×17-inch photograph or document and printing the same size image. If you do have a large photo or keepsake that you'd like to have digitized inexpensively, see if a scrapbook store in your area has installed this workstation.

In addition, you can print background papers—perhaps even printing directly on a textured material like fabric or cork, if it's thin enough for your printer. Delicate fabrics, tissue paper, and gauze can even be printed by first ironing them to ordinary freezer paper (the kind you buy in a roll like aluminum foil) and then cutting to fit the printer's paper tray. You can also use repositionable adhesive to adhere small tags and titles to a full-size paper sheet, sending it through the printer to print directly on the tags. You'll be able to lift the smaller paper pieces off the full-size sheet and then adhere them to your layout. You can also print digital embellishments like the tags shown in Figure 1.13 on a sheet of the desired paper, cut them out, and then adhere them to a traditional paper layout.

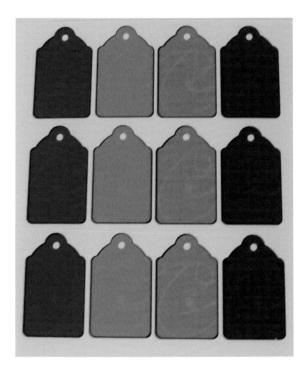

Figure 1.13

*Tags printed on paper stock
(courtesy of Amy Lemelin and Hawk Mountain Papers).*

The most convenient means of printing your digital layouts is a home-based inkjet printer. If you want to print layouts that are no larger than 8.5 inches×11 inches, a standard photo ink-jet printer will do the job. For larger layouts, you'd need a wide-carriage printer. The layout in Figure 1.14 was printed on a wide-format printer, the Hewlett Packard 9650, on 13×19 semi-gloss photo paper. One 12×12-inch copy and two 6×6-inch copies were produced on each sheet, resulting in layouts for three separate albums at an average cost of under $1.00 for each layout for ink and paper consumables. (We'll talk about printers more in Chapter 5.)

Figure 1.14

"Phyllis" digital layout by Sally Beacham.

Digital Cameras

Where would digital scrapbooking be without digital cameras? The price and availability of digital cameras has allowed the home user to produce excellent images in a jiffy, and that's opened the door for designing beautiful and expressive layouts on the computer as well. A digital camera is perhaps a scrapbooker's favorite tool—without photos, there's nothing to scrapbook (see Figure 1.15).

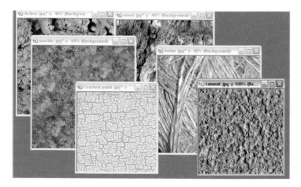

Figure 1.16

Close-up photographs of surface textures.

Figure 1.15

"Nature Photography with Canon Pro90" by Ron Lacey.

A digital camera is also helpful for the same reason as a scanner —you can create your own customized papers and embellishments from the objects around you. Everyone's garden yields great grasses, ferns, leaves, and blossoms that you can use to decorate a page. Everyday objects, such as the surface textures shown in Figure 1.16, can be photographed and used as decorative elements. Even interesting surfaces can quickly become your new background paper—think rust, cement, and peeling paint.

In Chapter 5 we'll take a look at some of the things you'll want to consider when shopping for a digital camera.

Graphics Tablet

Many people find a graphics tablet useful. This is a digitizing device that functions like a mouse and allows you to use a stylus to draw or write on a tablet surface. A graphics tablet can be a more natural method of drawing, but it does take a little practice to use it. If you're interested in learning more about graphics tablets, check out Wacom, the leading manufacturer of graphics tablets. Their Graphire line is less expensive than the Intuos line, and it is a good choice for a novice artist. (More information on Wacom's line of graphics tablets can be found at www.wacom.com.) We'll talk about graphic tablets more in Chapter 5.

Software

Let's look at some common types of software that the digital scrapbooker may find useful. We'll explore what's currently available and mention what we'll focus on in this book.

Useful Application Types

Many people begin digital scrapbooking by using a card-creator or print shop program. These applications often have special scrapbook templates built right in. They generally have some clip art included, and can be a good introductory program. You'll probably outgrow them quickly; they're usually quite limited in their flexibility.

Some companies offer special scrapbook creation applications. These applications also often have lots of included clip art, but they tend to be limited in tools and features and don't "grow" with the user. They do include lots of layout templates, so it might be worthwhile to try one out to investigate and learn good design tips. The art choices tend to be cartoonish, cutesy, or feminine, however. If these styles don't appeal to you, look elsewhere.

Painting applications such as Paint Shop Pro Photo and Photoshop Elements are the most common choice for digital scrapbooking. Paint programs—also called *image editors*—are usually distinguished by their ability to handle photographs well and to create new images using brush tools. Most advanced paint programs have features like image layers and the ability to use selections, masks, and special effects (more on all of this much later).

Photoshop is the mother of all paint applications, but it's also very expensive and difficult to learn. Almost any mid-price paint application contains enough tools and features to let the digital scrapbooker create anything they like—they are usually a tenth of the cost of Photoshop. For this reason, we won't present Photoshop-specific examples in this book (although the general discussion applies to Photoshop and just about any other image editor, too).

Corel Paint Shop Pro Photo, Adobe Photoshop Elements, Ulead's PhotoImpact, Corel PhotoPaint, and Serif's PhotoPlus are all good image editors, and they all have similar features—some work better or more easily than others, but all essentially can create the same layout. Microsoft's Digital Image Pro has also been very popular with scrappers. It's good for photos, but be advised that it lacks some essential tools for scrapbooking.

Illustration software, such as Xara X, Illustrator, and CorelDRAW, are good choices if all you would like to do is create your own embellishments from scratch and assemble your layouts. Illustration programs are considered "drawing" applications versus the "paint" applications previously mentioned. We won't work with these types of applications in this book. Many have limited or no means of editing and enhancing photographs, and that's an integral part of digital scrapbooking.

Desktop publishing programs, such as Microsoft Publisher, are excellent choices for page layouts because they're designed for print. But if you plan to use your digital layouts as image files only, this type of application wouldn't be a good choice. They also lack robust editing and image creation tools, so if you choose to use them for your layouts, you'll likely still want a good paint program to work with your photos and create embellishments.

Some page layout programs are integrated with other application types by the same software manufacturer. For example, Adobe's Photoshop, Illustrator, and InDesign use file types that are compatible and can be exported quickly from one application to another. This suite of applications is expensive, but if this type of package interests you, you might want to look at Serif's PhotoPlus, DrawPlus, and PagePlus applications. They're integrated as well and are reasonably priced.

The bottom line here is this: we recommend that if you're at all interested in creating your own scrapping components and editing your photos, you should have a moderately priced paint program such as Photoshop Elements or Paint Shop Pro Photo. Such an application will provide you with all the scrapping software you really need. And as you'll see later in the book, a paint program's functionality can be expanded further with plug-in filters.

Software Used in This Book

Since we'll concentrate on paint applications in this book, you can expect to see examples created with several different software applications. We'll use the current versions of the following applications throughout this book:

- **Adobe Photoshop Elements 5.0 and 6.0**
- **Corel Paint Shop Pro Photo X2**
- **Picasa**

Photoshop Elements and Paint Shop Pro Photo can be purchased at local stores, online at various resellers, and at the manufacturer's site. And Picasa is available for free online. Please check this book's Appendix A, "Resources," for Web site addresses.

And Away We Go!

TIME TO START SCRAPBOOKING.
Haul out those photos, and let's start creating some memories (see Figure 1.17).

Figure 1.17
"Wedding" layout by Lie Fhung.

Monroe County Fair BABY Queen

Monroe County Fair Queen

It may have only been a crown made from pipe cleaners, but to you it was pure gold! When your sister reached to take your crown from your head and try it on herself, you snatched it back and let her know it was yours! Royalty can apparently be very territorial. Mommy asked you to stand in front of the Fair Queen's car (for the week) and you were only too willing to pose as though it were your own. The contest was fun and you were adorable, but then it was back to real life. Your "reign" was short lived.

"Monroe County Fair Baby Queen" layout by Glenda Ketcham.

2

DigiScrapping 101

PICTURE YOURSELF SITTING AT YOUR COMPUTER, creating printable memory pages, using your own digital photos—and beautiful scrapbook components and embellishments. In this chapter, you'll learn the basics of page design and how to set up scrapbook pages in two popular applications. We'll talk about the single most important decision you'll have to make when you begin to design a layout—image resolution. We'll show you how to choose color schemes that complement your photos and how to use basic design principles to create your own memory masterpieces.

Figure 2.1

"Master Anthony" layout by Sally Beacham, using scrapbook components by Angela Cable, Roberta D'Achille, Lie Fhung, and Sally Beacham.

Last Things First: Is That Your Final Output?

IT MIGHT SEEM A LITTLE ODD to worry about the final stage of your layout first, but the way you intend to display it will determine how you make it. Traditionally, scrapbook pages are printed and placed in plastic sleeve protectors and then into albums. However, digital scrapbookers have other options to store and share their layouts. Page designs can be burned to CD or DVD, stored on other media for later printing, or perhaps never printed at all but rather viewed on a computer monitor or television screen. They can also be sized for display in a Web gallery, personal Web site, or multimedia slide show, or sent as an e-mail attachment.

Determining how you want the final product to be produced is sometimes a matter of cost or storage space. It's also possible to produce a design for display in *all* the ways discussed—perhaps you'll want a printed album for yourself, a slide show on CD for relatives, and a Web gallery for friends near and far to view. This is one of the advantages to digital scrapbooking; you can do all the creative work once and produce multiple versions in a snap.

Once you have a good idea how you'll use the page design, the most important question to answer is what size to make it? If you plan to print the design, you should have a specific album size in mind, whether it's 8.5×11 inch or 5×7 inch; but what if you want to send it via e-mail as well?

A good rule of thumb is to design for the largest size you might need, and then downsize from that image. Unless you think you will *never* want to print a specific design, always design for printed output, and then create any smaller images and Web graphics from the original print layout. In Figure 2.2, a 12×12-inch printable layout is resized to a Web graphic, sized at 600×600 pixels, suitable for e-mail or for posting in a Web picture gallery.

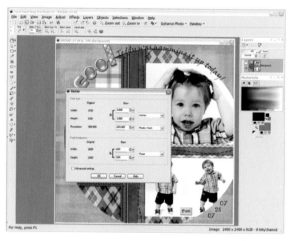

Figure 2.2

A print layout resized in Corel Paint Shop Pro Photo X2.

That Pesky Resolution Question

RESOLUTION IS A CONCEPT that stumps and stymies a lot of people. We'll discuss resolution as it relates to taking digital photographs and scanning film photos and memorabilia in Chapter 5, "Handling the Hardware," but now let's look at resolution for print and Web images. *Print resolution* refers to the capability of a printer to produce a finely-detailed image. A printer capable of high resolution will produce a better quality image than a low-resolution printer.

Printer resolution is referred to in dots per inch, or *dpi*, and this is a measurement of the density of ink drops that the printer will apply to paper. It's possible to set different printer resolutions for inkjet printers, but it's a function of the printer software and not the application you use to produce a layout. The higher the dpi a printer is capable of, the better quality print possible from that printer.

Image resolution is a completely different animal from print resolution. (In this book, we'll most often refer to image resolution.) Image resolution is the term used to describe the pixels that make up a computer-generated image. All digital images are made up of pixels and can be viewed on a computer monitor screen. The computer doesn't know inches or centimeters—it only knows pixels, and it doesn't even know how big those pixels are. A computer monitor displays a pixel based on its own settings. If an image is 800 pixels wide on one monitor, it's still 800 pixels wide on any other monitor, no matter how big it might look on the screen.

Here's the confusing part. You want to design a layout that prints in inches or centimeters, which are physical terms of measurement, but you need to design it on a computer monitor that only reads pixels. In addition, you need to create a fine balance between a good quality image that will print nicely (which equates to higher image resolution) and a digital file that is small enough in terms of bits and bytes for your computer system to work with comfortably.

Image resolution is defined as pixels per inch, or *ppi*. Ppi and dpi (printer resolution) are NOT the same thing, but are often used interchangeably. (This only adds to the confusion about image resolution, but let's try to keep it straight!) The more pixels per inch in an image, the higher the image resolution.

> **You may see information stating that Web graphics have or should have an image resolution of 72 or 96 ppi. Hogwash; that's hooey! A computer monitor doesn't care about inches, it only cares about pixels, so an 800-pixel wide image is always 800 pixels wide, no matter what image resolution it carries. That 800×800-pixel image will take up the same amount of bytes on your hard drive or Web server, too, no matter what its image resolution.**

For printer resolution, inches matter! You want your printer to be able to interpret what your monitor shows you and print your layout at your preferred size. So you've got to give the printer instructions, and those instructions are the image resolution value. Studies have shown that the human eye needs an image resolution of 180 to 220 pixels per inch for images that are viewed at arm's length (like most scrapbook layouts). This is also the most economical resolution to use for home inkjet printers. For images that will be viewed from a greater distance, such as a poster hanging on a wall, even lower resolution values are adequate. Image resolutions of higher than 200 ppi are only necessary for images printed on commercial off-set printers, like magazines and this book!

Another reason to consider the image resolution of your planned project carefully is that the higher the image resolution and intended final printed size, the larger the file size of the digital image. This means your computer will work much harder to create a 12×12-inch layout at 300 ppi resolution than the same 12×12-inch layout at 200 ppi. Three to four times harder, on average, in fact! If you have an older or less powerful computer, this difference in file size could be crucial—it could take minutes longer to render an effect on a 12×12-inch 300 ppi resolution layout than a comparable 200 ppi layout with the same print dimensions. *And* digital scrapbook component files take up three to four more times storage space on your computer at 300 ppi than those created for use at 200 ppi.

That 12×12-inch 300 ppi image has pixel dimensions of 3600×3600 pixels, while the 200 ppi image has pixel dimensions of only 2400×2400 pixels. That might not seem like a big deal, but as you add components and work with the layout in your image editor, the file size grows exponentially larger.

Your objective is to produce a layout that will print nicely but also not tax the computer's resources so much that you can't process images quickly. For this reason, all layouts in this book are produced at an image resolution of 200 pixels per inch, which produce an excellent quality print layout, while still creating reasonably small-sized image files to work on with the average home computer. All resources found on the accompanying DVD are also designed for and saved at 200 pixels per inch.

Faux Paper–Style or Not?

DIGITAL SCRAPBOOK LAYOUTS tend to fall into one of two distinct styles. One of these styles is a *faux paper* look—digital elements are created that simulate actual paper scrapbook embellishments with a high degree of realism. The more realistic something looks the better. This style of layout usually uses textured backgrounds that look like real paper, often adding simulated fibers and tags, photo mats, and other decorative elements. Roberta D'Achille made use of this style in the layout shown Figure 2.3.

Another style well-suited to digital scrapbooking is reminiscent of commercial print images; this style is commonly referred to as *graphic-design* style (see Figure 2.4). An example of this style is your favorite commercial print advertisement. Layouts created in this fashion don't incorporate a lot of simulated textures but focus on the photographs. Fonts play an important part in this style of layout—most of the decoration is different font styles and sizes. Word art, normally associated with Microsoft's Word application, is useful in creating large text banners and journal blocks.

Figure 2.3

"It's Not a Date" paper-style layout by Roberta D'Achille.

Figure 2.4

"Snuggled in Sunshine," a graphic design-style layout by Doris Castle.

You can even combine elements of both design styles, as in Figure 2.5. Here the designer has used graphic-style techniques (the text used as fill in the path the girls are walking, the de-saturated portions of the photo, and the journaling directly on the photo) with realistic components like the layered paper and stitching.

No matter which style you prefer, you'll find plenty of resources, including those on this book's DVD, to suit your needs.

Figure 2.5

"Sisters and Friends" by Doris Castle.

Common Layout Sizes

LAYOUTS CAN BE PRINTED in just about any imaginable size. How you'll print and store them will often determine the size you design, so let's discuss print sizes now.

12×12

A popular size for paper scrapbook albums is 12×12 inches, as shown in Figure 2.6. This size album is widely available at many different price points, often on sale at discount and craft stores. It's popular because a single page is large enough to allow for large photos, or many small ones. In addition, an open album produces a two-page spread, which can be used for panoramic photo displays or to create a theme.

The disadvantage to this size layout is that it can be difficult and expensive to print. You'll need a wide-carriage photo printer to print this size at home. It's possible to have these layouts printed professionally, but it can be an expensive proposition.

Some canny and frugal digital scrappers have their 12×12-inch layouts printed on 11×17-inch paper as a color photocopy at discount office supply stores. When trimmed, this photocopy yields an 11×11-inch layout, which can then be matted on standard 12×12-inch scrapbook cardstock, and then mounted in the album.

Figure 2.6

12×12 two-page layout created by Terry Maruca.

8.5×11

Another popular layout size, again a holdover from the paper scrapbook market, is 8.5×11 inches. Albums in that size are commonly available, and you can even find an album in landscape orientation, leaving more layout options. This layout size can often be printed on an inkjet printer and standard photocopiers. However, if the printer isn't capable of borderless (full-bleed) printing, you still may not get a true full-sized layout. If your printer can't produce borderless prints, any border can be trimmed and the layout can be mounted on 8.5 × 11-inch cardstock before placement in the album.

This size is also popular if you plan for most of your layouts to be viewed on a television screen or computer monitor. Since most monitor displays are landscape orientation, an 11×8.5 layout can be shown on-screen with less "wallpaper" bordering it on the sides. This is also an effective size/proportion to use for slide shows and Web galleries. (You should resize these layouts to smaller, more Web-friendly pixel dimensions. You'll learn how to do that later in this book.)

Figure 2.7

11×8.5 inch layout by Lie Fhung.

8×10

An 8×10-inch layout has a number of advantages. It can be printed on a home inkjet printer as well as photocopiers, but it can also be printed as an 8×10 photograph. Discount stores such as Wal-Mart have instant photo developing kiosks in their photo lab sections, so this size can be done quickly. The layout can also be printed at a regular photo lab or through an online photo developer, such as Shutterfly or Ofoto. Having a layout printed as a photo can often cost less than printing at home and is a good option if you don't have a photo-quality printer.

8×8 and Other Square Layouts

There are several variations on the 12×12-inch square theme; 8×8-inch and 6×6-inch layouts are common. The 8-inch square layout is popular because it's the largest square size that can be easily printed on standard 8.5×11-inch printer or photo paper with borders. You can easily find 8×8 and 6×6 albums at craft stores, specialized scrapbook stores, and other discount stores. The 6×6-inch size is especially good for albums commemorating an event, where you might choose to use one photo per page to highlight various activities or people at the event.

4×6 and Variations

Smaller snapshot size albums have become very popular. A 4×6-inch snapshot photograph can be printed very inexpensively at home or by the usual photo processors. These little albums make great gifts, and are the perfect size for little hands to hold. They can also be used for more unusual album concepts —like ABC albums, flashcard, or picture books for children. Another useful layout size is 5×7 inches—you can usually print two 5×7-inch layouts on a single 8.5×11-inch photo sheet (see Figure 2.8).

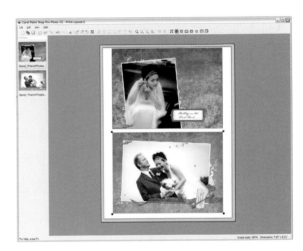

Figure 2.8

Print Layout feature of Paint Shop Pro Photo X2, two 5×7-inch layouts by Lie Fhung ready for printing.

Color Options

L ET'S TALK ABOUT A FEW BASICS of color design. Color, as it applies to paper scrapbooking, is added to paper and embellishments by the manufacturer in the form of pigments. Any color model representing pigmented color is referred to as a *subtractive color model*. In a subtractive color model, the color you see is determined by the color of light reflected from the pigments on the page. If you have paper-scrapped in the past, you may have used a color wheel to help you choose colors that work well together. Colors are designated as the following:

- **Primary.** A "pure" color that can't be made by combining any other colors. Red, yellow, and blue are primary colors in a subtractive color model.

- **Secondary.** Colors that are made by combining primary colors—for example, orange, green, and violet in a subtractive color model.

- **Tertiary.** Colors that are made by combining a primary and secondary color— for example, red-orange and blue-violet in a subtractive color model. There are six tertiary colors, resulting in 12 colors total in the color wheel with which you may be familiar from an art class or paper scrapping.

Additionally, each color may be modified further by adding white, black, or various amounts of gray. Colors created by adding these neutral pigments are called tints, tones, and shades:

- **Tint.** Color plus white.

- **Shade.** Color plus black.

- **Tone.** Color mixed with various amounts of gray.

Once you understand color model basics, you can use color harmonies to create schemes in your layouts. Color harmonies are groups of related or complementary colors that will work together to create a pleasing arrangement. Some common color harmonies, as shown in Figure 2.9, are

- **Monochromatic.** Shades, tints, and tones of a single color.

- **Complementary.** Color used with the color directly opposite it on the color wheel. The complement of red on a traditional color wheel is green.

- **Analogous.** Color used with the two tertiary colors adjacent to it on a color wheel. Red-orange, red, and red-yellow (or their tones, tints, and shades) would be an example of an analogous scheme.

- **Triadic.** Three colors that are equidistant from each other on the color wheel. Blue-green, yellow-orange, and red-purple are triadic colors—any tone, tint, or shade of these colors may be used to create the scheme.

- **Tetradic.** Four colors that are equidistant from each other on the color wheel.

- **Split-Complementary.** A color and the analogous colors to the right and left of that color's complement on the color wheel. Red, blue-green, and yellow-green are a split-complementary scheme.

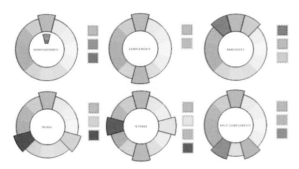

Figure 2.9

Examples of color harmonies, courtesy of Color Schemer Studio.

Computer monitors use a different color model, one based on emitted light rather than reflected light. In this model, the primary colors are red, green, and blue. This creates a bit of a dilemma if you're already familiar with the color model and wheel used by paper scrapbookers to create color schemes—you can still use the same concepts for various color harmonies, but you'll work with an RGB model instead of an RYB one.

So, what's a digital scrapper to do, if selecting coordinated color schemes using a computer isn't as easy as with paper and pigments? You can use a separate application to help you find good color schemes. Color Schemer Online (www.colorschemer.com/online.html) is a free Web service that will give you coordinating colors in either RGB or a *hexadecimal code* (or HEX, the color code you need when working with Web page colors).

The tutorial at www.colorschemer.com/tutorial2.html shows you how to use this type of color model to create traditional schemes.

The same site offers Color Schemer Studio, which adds color wheel functionality and helps you pick several design schemes (see Figure 2.10). There's a free 15-day trial of Color Schemer Studio on the resource DVD for this book. This is an excellent utility application for digital scrapbookers. It allows you to create harmonious color schemes (see Figure 2.11), save favorite color swatches, analyze how color schemes will look as background and text colors, and use the Suggested Colors tab shown in Figure 2.12 to show how various color schemes will look as part of a Web page (which also works beautifully to suggest how those same colors will work in a digital layout). A triadic color scheme based on the violet base color in the left pane is shown in Figure 2.13. In the right pane, you can see a list of favorite colors created from various color harmonies and that violet color.

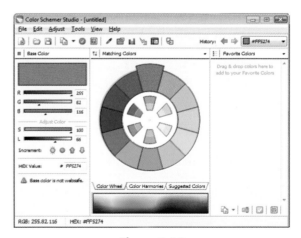

Figure 2.10

Color Wheel panel in Color Schemer Studio 1.5.

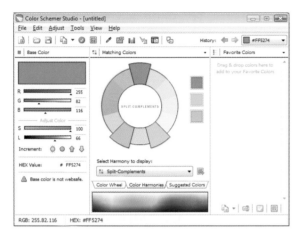

Figure 2.11

Color Harmonies tab of Color Schemer Studio 1.5.

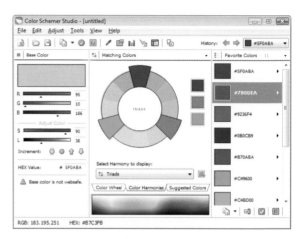

Figure 2.13

Triadic color scheme and Favorites color swatches in Color Schemer Studio 1.5.

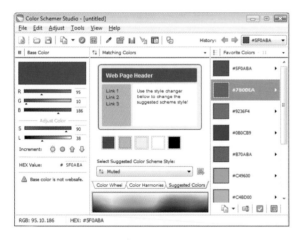

Figure 2.12

Suggested Colors panel in Color Schemer Studio 1.5.

Once you've selected the colors you want to include in your layout, you can find their RGB or HEX color values in the Favorite Colors pane or in the bottom status bar (for the base color only). You'll need those numbers when you choose the colors in the image editor you'll use to create your layout. Color Schemer Studio can also export the Favorite Colors as well as Color Wheel, Color Mixer, and Color History colors to an Adobe Photoshop color palette, an HTML color table file, a CSS style sheet file, or to a GIF image, which gives you an easy way to store and access color scheme palettes when you start designing your layout.

Figure 2.14

Color Palette exported from Color Studio 1.5.

There are other online resources to help you create color harmonies. Another good free resource is available from Adobe at http://kuler.adobe.com/#. There's a terrific gallery of harmony swatches to inspire you, too.

You can use a software utility to create harmonious color schemes, trust your own eyes, or use other methods. Paper scrapbookers often use ordinary paint chips, available at most hardware and paint supply stores, to reference when creating pleasing color arrangements. Digital scrappers can use these paint chips as well—just scan them in and save the image, using it as a mini-palette of color when choosing image colors.

Color schemes can be seen all around you—in fabrics and everyday objects around the home, in nature (for who's a better colorist, the computer or Mother Nature herself?), and in the photos you use. Try to choose a color scheme that will complement the photos and not compete with them.

Using Quick Pages, Overlays, and Sketches

SOMETIMES YOU HAVE PHOTOS to work with and no ideas. You may need a little help creating an effective layout that positions the photos in a pleasing manner or the design concept.

Digital scrapbookers make good use of

- **Templates.** Pre-made layouts just waiting for you to drop your photos in.

- **Overlays.** These add special effects over existing photos and papers.

- **Sketches.** Design notes to help you create well-balanced layouts.

Quick Pages are pre-made album pages with all design elements in place, just waiting for you to add your own photos.

You'll find Quick Pages from many designers on the resource DVD accompanying this book. Just open the template in your image editor, open and resize the photos you want to use, and copy/paste them into the template. The 12×12-inch layout in Figure 2.15 was made with a Quick Page you can find on this book's DVD.

Quick Page or Whatchamacallit?

We'll use the term *Quick Page* throughout this book, but you'll find them referred to at different scrapbook shops and online sites by various terms. Plopper and Quick Stick are just two of the alternate terms you may hear, but the terms mean the same thing—a pre-made layout page with all the design elements fixed in place, ready to add photos. Quick Pages come in two flavors—PNG files, to which you add photos UNDER the page in cutout areas, and JPEG files, where the photos are placed on top of the pre-made page.

Figure 2.15

Layout produced from "Cherished" Plopper, by Marcee Duggar at www.digitalscrapbookplace.com.

A *template* is generally considered to be a blueprint for a layout. Figure 2.16 shows a template image that can be found on this book's accompanying DVD.

Figure 2.16

"Inaspot" Quick Page template by Lauren Bavin at www.digitalscrapbookplace.com.

Figure 2.17 shows the same scrapbook template, with "filled" areas, photos in place, and additional embellishments added. Templates can be used quickly to achieve great results, and are often available for free at many digital scrapbook Web sites. There are countless more templates for purchase on CD or by electronic download for a reasonable cost as well.

Overlays add special image effects to photos, mats, or layout backgrounds. Figure 2.18 shows an overlay image that can be used to add an antique frame effect over a photograph in Paint Shop Pro Photo X2. The overlay also adds some distressed-look effects to the underlying background paper.

Figure 2.17

Completed layout using "Inaspot" template and "Blossom Blush" kit, both by Lauren Bavin, and "Ink Swirls" Alpha by Christine Beasley, from this book's DVD.

Figure 2.18

"Love" overlay by Lisa Carter at www.digitalscrapbookplace.com.

By adding the overlay on a background paper and an antique photo, and then adding some page embellishments and text, you can quickly create a beautiful, personalized layout like the one in Figure 2.19.

Figure 2.19

Completed layout using "Love" overlay by Lisa Carter," "Blossom Blush" page kit by Lauren Bavin, and "Evergreen Tapestry Alpha" by Jennifer Maceyunas, all from this book's DVD.

Another type of resource that can be used for inspiration, is a sketch. Sketches are just little blueprints for picture or object placement. The concept of sketches originated as design plans for paper scrapbook layouts, but they work equally well for digital layouts. You can find sketches in many scrapbook magazines, and many Web sites devoted to digital scrapbooking have sketches available for free as well. Figure 2.20 shows the online gallery at www.digitalscrapbookplace.com with many types of sketches to help you plan your own layouts.

Resizing Pre-made Layouts

Templates and pre-made layouts designed for 8.5×11-inch layouts are often flexible enough to be used at the 8×10-inch size as well (and vice versa). The templates made for 12×12-inch layouts don't resize as well for the rectangular layouts, but they work beautifully for smaller square layouts.

Now that you've learned about different sizes, styles, and types of layout design, it's time to picture yourself creating your own masterpiece in our next chapter.

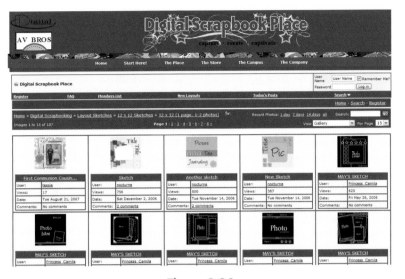

Figure 2.20

Layout Sketch gallery at Digital Scrapbook Place.

Figure 2.21

"Next Top Model" layout by Lauren Bavin.

ENTRY PERMIT
APRIL 30 2004
IMMIGRATION
SERVICE

PASSPORT

TO SEE
THE WORLD

VISAS

permission to visit
- Las Vegas, Nevada
- Hoover Dam
- Grand Canyon

*must be accompanied
by loved ones at all
times*

VISAS
Peter Beacham
Ann Beacham

IMMIGRATION
7 JUN 05
ARRIVAL

"Permission to See America" layout by Sally Beacham. Scrapbook Plopper by Lauren Bavin.

3

Creating Your First Layout

PICTURE YOURSELF SHOWING off a beautiful scrapbook to your friends and family. It's filled with special photographs, enhanced with attractive backgrounds and embellishments, and made meaningful with your own thoughts and memories recorded on each page. You'll need some basic tools and resources. Let's get started creating that scrapbook right now! (See Figure 3.1.)

Figure 3.1

"Handyman" by Lie Fhung.

Prepping Your Photos

L ATER IN THIS BOOK, you'll work in depth with your digital photos, but for now you'll learn some simple but very useful techniques for preparing your photos for use in your layouts. Whether you've downloaded photos from a digital camera, or you are planning to use scanned photographs, you will likely need to crop, resize, or straighten some of your images.

A word of caution before you begin—ALWAYS work on duplicates of the original digital files. If you make a mistake and inadvertently save it over the original, you may not be able to recover the original photo. To be safe, always make a duplicate copy and close the original before you begin to work. The easiest way to do this is as follows:

- In Paint Shop Pro Photo X2, with the photo open in the workspace, go to Window > Duplicate, or press SHIFT+D. This will create a new image exactly like the original. Close the original with no changes and begin work on the copy.

- In Photoshop Elements 5.0 or 6.0, with the photo open in the workspace, go to File > Duplicate. This will create a new image on the workspace. Close the original and begin work on the new image.

Cropping a Photo

Cropping a photo means to remove portions of the photo. Perhaps you want to bring the shot in closer on the subject and eliminate image detail at the outer edges. Maybe you'd like to cut out just a piece of the photo to highlight it. Sometimes you just want to get rid of that stray dog who wandered into the frame of your otherwise perfect photo! Figure 3.2 shows an example of a photo with unwanted image information cropped away, using Paint Shop Pro Photo X2.

Click to apply crop

Click to apply crop and create new image

Original

Finished crop

Figure 3.2

Original photo, duplicate photo with Crop Tool active, and result in Paint Shop Pro Photo X2.

Cropping versus Resizing

All digital photos begin with defined pixel dimensions. Cropping and resizing can both change those dimensions, but they do so in different ways.

Cropping removes image detail and information, resulting in smaller pixel dimensions. Any image information that remains in the photo is the same physical size as it originally was, but the photo is smaller because some of it has been removed, just as if you had used a paper trimmer to remove edges of a printed photo.

Resizing also results in smaller pixel dimensions (if you are down-sizing, of course!). However, no image information or detail is removed. The photo is simply made smaller by reducing the overall size of all the image information contained in the photo. In effect, you "shrink" the image!

Figure 3.4

The Crop Tool icon in Paint Shop Pro Photo X2.

Interchangeable Applications

Although you'll work primarily with Photoshop Elements 5.0, Elements 6.0, and Paint Shop Pro Photo X2 in this book, you can usually accomplish most tasks we present in any image editor (and often other types of applications, too!). The terminology and tool set may be different, but the concepts are the same. Whatever application you choose to use, it should have the ability to import graphics and photos, to move objects on the background, and to resize objects as needed.

Your weapon of choice in most image editors is the Crop Tool. Figure 3.3 shows the toolbar icon for the Crop Tool in Photoshop Elements 5.0. Figure 3.4 shows the same tool in Paint Shop Pro Photo X2.

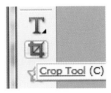

Figure 3.3

The Crop Tool icon on the toolbar in Adobe Photoshop Elements 5.0.

With the photo you want to work with open in the editor's workspace, activate the Crop Tool by clicking on its icon in the toolbar. Define the area of the photo that you want to retain by clicking on a corner starting point and dragging to the opposite corner of the area you want to retain. Figure 3.5 shows a scanned photo with the crop area set to eliminate the white border edge of the original photo in Photoshop Elements 5.0. Click on the green check mark. This will apply the crop and remove the unwanted areas.

Figure 3.5

Crop area set in Photoshop Elements 5.0.

The Crop Tool in Paint Shop Pro works the same way—click on the tool, drag out the crop area you want to define, and apply the crop by clicking on the green check mark (see Figure 3.6).

Click to apply crop and
create new image

Click and drag to
move side of crop area

Click to apply crop

Figure 3.6

Crop area defined in Paint Shop Pro Photo X2.

Paint Shop Pro Photo X2 has a nice feature added in this version. It's possible to apply a crop and immediately create it as a new image in the workspace, while retaining the original in the workspace as well. Figure 3.7 shows where to locate this feature in the floating crop toolbar that becomes visible on the image when the Crop Tool is active. It's also available in the Tool options for the Crop Tool. This is particularly handy if you have scanned several photos at the same time and need to separate them to use them individually, as shown in Figure 3.8.

Crop as new image

Figure 3.7

Crop as New Image feature in Paint Shop Pro Photo X2.

Figure 3.8

Photo cropped as new image in Paint Shop Pro Photo X2.

Resizing a Photo

Once you've cropped your photos to your satisfaction, you may need to resize them for use in your scrapbook layout. Most consumer-level digital cameras, with the image size set on its Fine or High quality setting, will produce a photograph large enough to be printed as an 8×10-inch print or larger. That size is probably too big for use in your planned layout, so it's helpful to resize those photos before you try to use them in your layouts. You can still modify that size in the layout itself, as you will see later. But let's get your photos to a manageable size first, shall we?

Let's begin with the premise that you are designing your layouts at 200 ppi, and that you will need photos of a certain print size within those layouts. If you work with a layout that is intended to be printed as a 12×12-inch layout, you will want the photos you use to be proportional to that. A good rule of thumb is to resize photos to be approximately 25–33% of the finished layout size in their largest dimension (either height or width). If you plan for one or more photos to be larger, you might want to resize that photo to approximately 50% of the layout size in its largest dimension.

In Photoshop Elements 5.0, with a photo open in the workspace, go to Image > Resize > Image Size or press ALT+CTRL+I. Make sure the Resolution is set to the resolution value you're working at (200 ppi in this book). You can choose to resize by changing the pixel dimensions or by setting the print size you'd like. Figure 3.9 shows the Image Size dialog box in Photoshop Elements 5.0. Make sure the check box for Constrain Proportions remains checked—this will allow you to change only the height or width and have Elements automatically set the other dimension to a value that is proportional to the one you set.

Why Resize?

Why do you need to resize your photos before you begin to create the layout? The larger in file size an image is, the harder your computer has to work to process it. As you open and work with multiple images, your computer may slow down. It's more effective to give your computer smaller file sizes to work with, so by resizing photos before you place them in a layout, you minimize the work load of the computer.

You can still modify the photo size inside the layout, but any large scale changes should be made to the photos before you start assembling the layout.

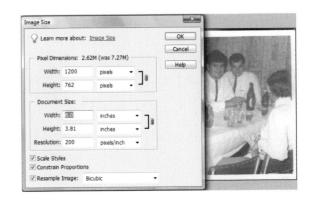

Figure 3.9

Image Size dialog in Photoshop Elements 5.0.

Paint Shop Pro Photo X2 has a similar tool to resize photos—with an image open in the workspace, go to Image > Resize or press SHIFT+S. This will open the Resize dialog (see Figure 3.10). Set the Resolution to the value you want to work with (200 ppi for our purposes), and then choose either print or pixel values to set the new dimensions. You will notice that if you change the Print dimensions, the Pixel dimensions will automatically change, and vice versa.

Now that you've got some basic photo editing tasks taken care of, let's get to that layout!

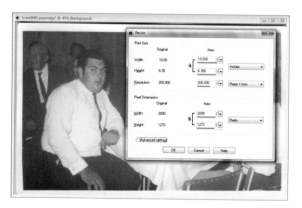

Figure 3.10

Resize dialog in Paint Shop Pro Photo X2.

Creating a Quick Page Layout

I N THIS SECTION, YOU'LL create a layout
using a pre-made Quick Page and your own
photograph. You're going to use a Quick Page
designed by Lie Fhung that can be found on the
book's DVD—the image titled Ztampf_QuickPage_
PaintingKit_02.png, located in the Designer Kits
section. This is a 2400×2400-pixel image designed
to print as large as 12×12 inches. Open this image
and the photograph of your choice in your image
editor. In Figure 3.11, both images are open in
Paint Shop Pro Photo X2, and we've already resized
the photo to be 8 inches wide.

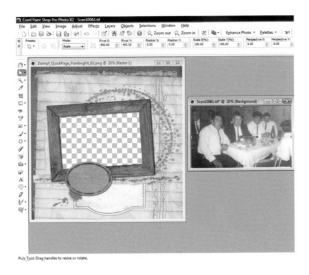

Figure 3.11

*Quick Page and photo images open on workspace
in Paint Shop Pro Photo X2.*

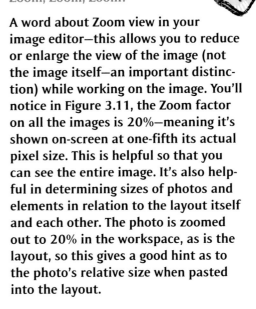

Zoom, Zoom, Zoom!

**A word about Zoom view in your
image editor—this allows you to reduce
or enlarge the view of the image (not
the image itself—an important distinc-
tion) while working on the image. You'll
notice in Figure 3.11, the Zoom factor
on all the images is 20%—meaning it's
shown on-screen at one-fifth its actual
pixel size. This is helpful so that you
can see the entire image. It's also helpful in determining sizes of photos and
elements in relation to the layout itself
and each other. The photo is zoomed
out to 20% in the workspace, as is the
layout, so this gives a good hint as to
the photo's relative size when pasted
into the layout.**

You need to learn a few more editing basics now.
As is common in most Windows applications, the
Copy and Paste functions are very useful. In Paint
Shop Pro and Photoshop Elements, these functions
can be found in the Edit menu (see Figures 3.12
and 3.13).

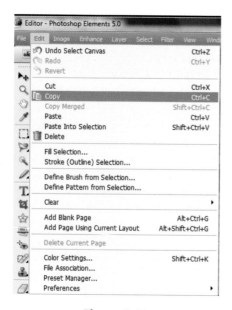

Figure 3.12

Edit menu in Photoshop Elements 5.0.

Figure 3.13

Edit menu in Paint Shop Pro Photo X2.

Working with Layers

You can copy images or parts of images and paste them into other images in various ways. But first, you need to learn about one of the most important features of any good image editor—the layers concept.

Think of the Layers feature as layers of paper, photos and embellishments on a paper scrapbook layout. In a paper layout, you can move these objects around the background paper until you are satisfied. If a piece of paper rests on top of a photo, the photo is covered and can't be seen. The concept is the same with image layers. Anything in a layer that is not transparent may cover another object below it, rendering it invisible unless the object is moved or another action causes it to be visible. Applications that use a layers model are flexible for the digital scrapbooker. Please refer to the Help files of your image editor for more information on image layers.

Figure 3.14 shows the Layers palette in Paint Shop Pro Photo X2. The Quick Page image shown has one layer. You'll add more soon!

Photoshop Elements has a Layers palette, too. Figure 3.15 shows our photo image with the Layers palette in Photoshop Elements 5.0.

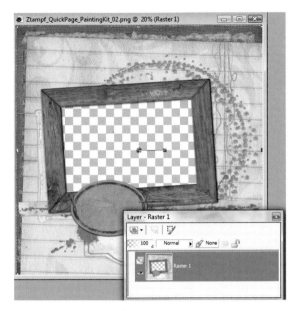

Figure 3.14

Layers palette in Paint Shop Pro Photo X2.

Figure 3.15

Layers palette in Photoshop Elements 5.0.

Notice that the layer name is titled Background. In both Paint Shop Pro and Photoshop Elements, images without transparency are created on a Background layer. Background layers do not allow the user to utilize all tools and features available, so often you need to change that layer type. In Photoshop Elements, to change the background layer to a regular layer, go to Layer > New > Layer from Background. The dialog seen in Figure 3.16 will open. You can rename the layer anything you like or leave it named Layer 0. You can also change the layer name by double-clicking directly on the title Background in the Layers palette, which opens the New Layer dialog, too.

Figure 3.16

New Layer dialog in Photoshop Elements 5.0.

Paint Shop Pro uses a similar method to change the Background layer to a regular layer. With an image open, go to Layers > Promote Background Layer. This will change the layer title to Raster 1. You can change the Background layer by double-clicking on that layer title in the Layers palette as well. The Layer Properties dialog box will open. Type in the name you choose or leave it set to the default Raster 1 title, as in Figure 3.17.

Figure 3.17

Layer Properties dialog in Paint Shop Pro Photo X2.

Layers can be moved, deleted, modified in many ways, and even made invisible. Using layers allows you to move photographs, papers, mats, embellishments, and text freely in the layout, even if you have added other components. Layers are the scrapbooker's best friends! Let's add one now.

Make sure the photo image is the active image in the workspace. You can do this by just clicking on the image's title bar. If you are using Photoshop Elements, go to Select > All or press CTRL+A.

Once you've selected the photo, you will see a blinking dotted line surrounding the entire photo. This is referred to as a *selection marquee* and denotes the existence of an active selection. In Paint Shop Pro, this step is not necessary. Just click on the photo title bar in the workspace to make the photo active.

Go to Edit > Copy or press CTRL+C to copy the selected photo to the Windows Clipboard. Now click on the Quick Page image to make it the active image in the workspace. Go to Edit > Paste. This will paste the photo as a new layer above the Quick Page image. See Figure 3.18 to view the image and the Layers palette in Photoshop Elements 5.0.

Photo layer pasted into
Quick Page image

Photo layer added

Original layer

Photo layer active

Photo layer dragged under
Quick Page layer

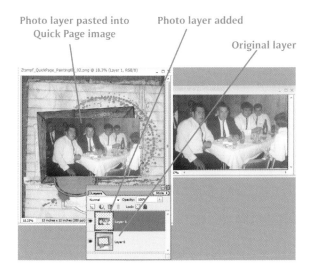

Figure 3.18

*Photo layer pasted into Quick Page image
in Photoshop Elements 5.0.*

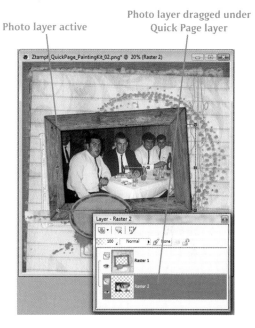

Figure 3.19

*Photo layer dragged under Quick Page layer
in Paint Shop Pro Photo X2.*

The process is the same in Paint Shop Pro. Once the photo is pasted into the Quick Page image, you can close the photo image in the workspace. Make a habit of closing component images as soon as you no longer need them—it will leave your workspace less cluttered and minimize the workload of your computer at the same time.

The photo is now positioned on top of the Quick Page—but it would look much better if the photo were placed *in* the frame. You can do this quickly by re-ordering the layers in the Layers palette. Click on the layer title of the photo layer (Raster 2 if you are using Paint Shop Pro, Layer 1 in Photoshop Elements). Hold down the left mouse button and drag the layer title *under* the Quick Page layer in the Layers palette. Refer to Figure 3.19 to see this action.

As you can see in Figure 3.19, the portions of the photo layer that are under the opaque portions of the Quick Page layer are hidden. They are still part of the image, as can be seen in the layer thumbnail image that is shown on the Layers palette.

Moving Objects Within the Layout

The photo layer is active, as indicated by the blue highlight showing on the layer title. The photo in the image is also surrounded by a marquee, indicating it's the active layer. This marquee is different from a blinking selection marquee —this one indicates that a tool is active. In this case, it's the Pick Tool in Paint Shop Pro Photo X2 (see Figure 3.20) or the Move Tool in Photoshop Elements (see Figure 3.21).

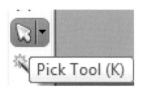

Figure 3.20

Pick Tool icon in Paint Shop Pro Photo X2.

Figure 3.21

Move Tool icon in Photoshop Elements 5.0.

The Move or Pick Tool is used to move the layer contents, as well as rotate, resize, and apply other transformations. In this case, we'd like to rotate the photo slightly so that it better lines up with the built-in frame on the Quick Page.

The Move or Pick Tool marquee has several control points along its borders and at its center. The center control point is used to move the object—click on it and drag the object to the desired position. The object can be resized by clicking and dragging any of the control points on the edges of the marquee. Click and drag on the top or bottom edge to change the height or on the sides to change the width. If you'd like to change both dimensions at the same time (and proportionately) click on a corner control point and drag.

Figure 3.22 shows the Move Tool in Photoshop Elements 5.0. The rotation handle extends from the bottom center control point. Hover your mouse cursor over this handle till you see a curved double-headed arrow—then click and drag the handle to rotate the selected object. Once you are satisfied with the rotation, position, and size of the object, click the green check mark to apply the transformation. You can also cancel the transformation by clicking the red Null sign.

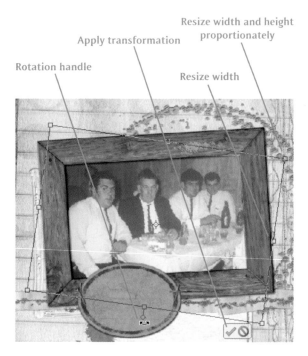

Figure 3.22

Move Tool in Photoshop Elements 5.0.

Paint Shop Pro Photo X2's Pick Tool works in a similar fashion. Side control points change the height or width dimensions, while corner control points can be used to change both simultaneously. Changing both dimensions proportionately is also referred to as *maintaining the aspect ratio* of the image or object.

The rotation handle for the Pick Tool can be found as an extension of the center control point in Paint Shop Pro. Hover your mouse cursor over this handle until the cursor turns to two curved arrows, then click and drag to rotate the object. Notice that even though the edges of the photograph in Figure 3.23 are hidden by the Quick Page frame above it, the Pick Tool marquee indicates where those edges are, so you will be able to align the object as desired.

Center control point

Rotation handle cursor

Corner control point

Figure 3.23

Pick Tool in Paint Shop Pro Photo X2.

Adding Text to a Layout

Once you've aligned and positioned the photo as you like, it's time to add some text to the Quick Page layout. Most applications have a special Text Tool that allows the use of fonts, colored text, special attributes like italic, bold, or underlined text, vertical or curved text, and special effects. Figures 3.24 and 3.25 show the Text Tool icon in both Paint Shop Pro and Photoshop Elements, which can be found on their respective toolbars.

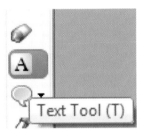

Figure 3.24

*Text Tool icon in
Paint Shop Pro Photo X2.*

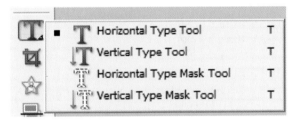

Figure 3.25

Text Tool icon in Photoshop Elements 5.0.

**Paint Shop Pro's Pick and
Move Tools**

Paint Shop Pro Photo X2 has a Pick Tool, which you've been using to move and modify objects. Paint Shop Pro also has a separate Move Tool, not to be confused with the Pick Tool. The Move Tool moves objects on layers, as does the Pick Tool, but it does not have any transformation capabilities, so you can't resize or otherwise modify the object with the Move Tool.

Activate the Text Tool in Paint Shop Pro by clicking on its icon in the toolbar. Once the tool is active, observe the Tool options for this tool, shown in Figure 3.26. There are options for choosing font, size, style, alignment, direction, and several other advanced attributes.

Two important features to observe in Paint Shop Pro—the Create As mode of Vector and the ability to set a stroke width. Vector text is a type of text that allows you to modify many of its attributes at a later date, sometimes even after you've saved, closed, and re-opened the layout file. It's always a good idea to create text as vector.

Setting a stroke width means that you can create text that is outlined in one color, but filled in another. In Paint Shop Pro, you can even create strokes and fills in gradients or patterns, which gives you great flexibility when creating titles and journaling.

You'll be working with the Horizontal Text Tool in Photoshop Elements. Figure 3.27 shows the options for text with this tool. Some features you may find useful are the Warped text option, which creates text in a shape, and the Styles options. *Styles* are special effects that can be used to make text look like it's embossed, beveled, shadowed, or textured.

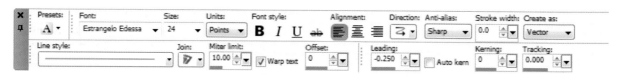

Figure 3.26

Text Tool options in Paint Shop Pro Photo X2.

Figure 3.27

Text Tool options in Photoshop Elements 5.0.

Working with Color in a Layout

Let's learn about choosing colors to work with in your application. You'll need to set a *background color* and a *foreground color*.

> ***Background color*** and ***foreground color*** are terms used in most paint programs to denote two separate color swatches that are active for use in the application. The terms are arbitrary and could just as easily be called "Color 1" and "Color 2" or "Bob" and "Fred." The terms exist to allow you to differentiate between the two color choices, and different tools and features may make use of one or both of these colors. In most of the New Image dialogs described thus far, the currently assigned background color is one of the image background options available when creating the new image.

In Paint Shop Pro Photo X2, the background and foreground color swatches are located near the Color Picker in the Materials palette (see Figure 3.28).

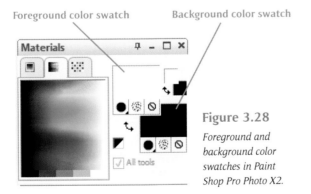

Foreground color swatch

Background color swatch

Figure 3.28

Foreground and background color swatches in Paint Shop Pro Photo X2.

In Photoshop Elements 5.0, the background and foreground color swatches are located at the bottom of the toolbar. In Figure 3.29, you can see the small icon to swap the colors as well, which can be very handy.

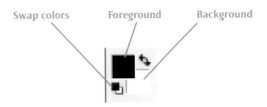

Swap colors Foreground Background

Figure 3.29

Foreground and background color swatches in Photoshop Elements.

Change the color of a swatch by clicking directly on it. This action will open a Color Picker, and you can choose any color you like. Set both background and foreground colors in this fashion. In addition, you may find other ways of setting color options in your application, so refer to the Help files or manual for additional options.

In Paint Shop Pro, it's also possible to set a swatch to Null, which means no color is associated with it. This can be very handy if you'd like to make outlined text with no fill so that the background beneath the text shows through. There's also a Swap Colors option in Paint Shop Pro (see Figure 3.30).

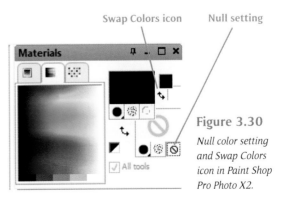

Swap Colors icon Null setting

Figure 3.30

Null color setting and Swap Colors icon in Paint Shop Pro Photo X2.

Once you've chosen two colors to work with, you can add some text to the Quick Page layout.

To apply text to your layout, click on the Quick Page layer in the Layers palette so that you are working on the top layer of the image. Otherwise, you might actually place your text under the Quick Page layer, and it may not be visible.

Set the colors of your choice in the foreground and background color swatches. Activate the Text Tool by clicking on its icon in the toolbar. Set the attributes of your choice (font, style, size, alignment), and type the text on the image. You will be able to position it after you create it.

As you apply the text, a separate layer will be created. (In Paint Shop Pro, this layer will be named Vector 1 unless you choose to rename it. In Photoshop Elements, the layer will be named by the text applied.) Click OK to apply the text.

The text will have an active marquee around it, which you can use to resize or re-position the text, just as you learned to do with the Pick Tool earlier. If you need to re-position the text on the layout, click and drag it to the desired position. Figure 3.31 shows text created in Paint Shop Pro, as well as the Layers palette, the Tool Options dialog for the text, and the Text Entry dialog.

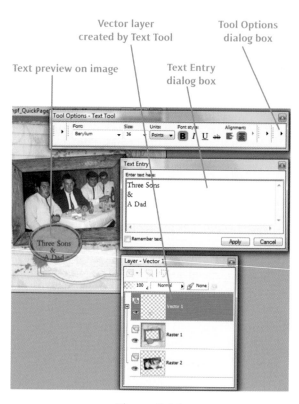

Vector layer created by Text Tool

Tool Options dialog box

Text preview on image

Text Entry dialog box

Figure 3.31

Text Options and Text Entry dialog boxes in Paint Shop Pro Photo X2.

Fonts, Beautiful Fonts!

The fonts used in Figure 3.31 are Beryllium and Effloresce, from Larabie Fonts, and can be found on this book's resource DVD in the Fonts section.

There are thousands of fonts available as freeware on the Internet. Fonts are often included in software packages or clipart packages and can be purchased singly or in collections.

If you're using Photoshop Elements 5.0, text application is similar. Activate the Text Tool icon on the toolbar, and then choose the text attributes you'd like. Type the text, and it will automatically be applied to the image. If you want to move the text, highlight it by dragging the mouse cursor along the text string, and click at any corner of the highlighted text. Drag the text to desired position. Figure 3.32 shows text applied in Photoshop Elements and several text layers created in the Layers palette.

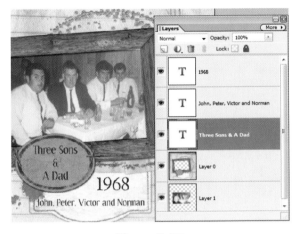

Figure 3.32

Text applied in Photoshop Elements 5.0.

Figure 3.33

Layer style applied to text in Photoshop Elements 5.0.

Special effects can easily be applied to text in Photoshop Elements. Highlight the text layer you'd like to add an effect to, and click on the Styles icon in the Tool options. In Figure 3.33, we've applied a Simple Pillow Emboss to the text on the tag under the photo.

That's it! (See Figure 3.34.) Creating a Quick Page layout is fast and easy, once you've mastered a few basic tools. Some Quick Pages are flexible enough to be flipped or rotated, so you can get multiple uses from the same page. You can also add additional embellishments to vary the design. If you like this design, there are matching components included in the Designer Kits section of the book's DVD.

Figure 3.34

Completed Quick Page layout
(Quick Page courtesy of Lie Fhung and Ztampf!).

Creating a Layout Using Pre-made Components

Now that you've learned the basic tools you need for layout construction, let's assemble a layout using pre-made components from scrapbook kits. Kits are comprised of co-coordinating papers, embellishments, and occasionally alphabet sets to give you maximum flexibility while maintaining an overall theme and color scheme. You can find many kits on this book's DVD by some outstanding designers.

There are two ways to start a new layout image:

- Open a pre-made background paper in your image editor.

- Create a new image of the size you prefer for the finished result and build upon it.

Most applications have an entry under the File menu to create a new image. Adobe Photoshop Elements 5.0 allows you to name the image, choose height and width in inches or other unit of measure, as well as define the image resolution in pixels per inch or centimeters (see Figure 3.35). You also have a choice of background color for the initial image—White, Transparent, or Background Color. "Background" refers to the Background Color setting in the Tool palette for this application.

You can also choose from a number of pre-defined image layouts in the Preset drop-down list, accessed by clicking the arrow to the right of the list title. In Figure 3.36, you'll see an available preset image size for 8×10.

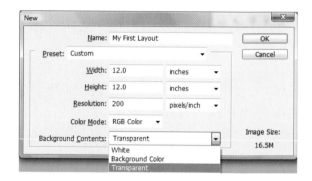

Figure 3.35

The New image dialog box in Adobe Photoshop Elements 5.0.

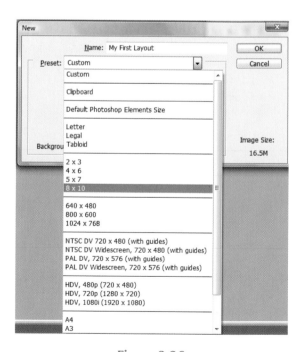

Figure 3.36

Preset image sizes available in Photoshop Elements 5.0.

This setting has an automatic resolution setting of 300 pixels per inch, so if you choose that setting, you may want to choose a lower resolution for the image. Just type the resolution you want in the dialog box, and click OK. You've just started a new image in Photoshop Elements.

You'll notice there aren't any presets for 8.5×11-inch or 12×12-inch layouts in Photoshop Elements 5.0. There's another option to open a new image, however, that does offer those preset sizes. Go to File > Create > Photo Layout. As shown in Figure 3.37, several standard scrapbook album sizes are available. In addition, you can choose a layout style, which you can modify later, and a choice of No Theme or several simple themes.

Beware the Hidden Resolution Gotchas!

Photoshop Elements 5.0 has several easy-to-use features to create layouts, but the resolution is pre-determined and can trip you up. The resolution for photo layouts created using the File > Create command is set at 220 ppi, which creates an odd-sized layout of 2640×2640 pixels.

If you use standard scrapbook kit components, paper and embellishment sizes will not be the same scale as the layout.

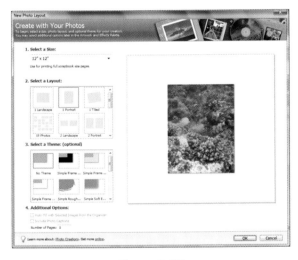

Figure 3.37

New Photo Layout dialog in Photoshop Elements 5.0.

For Paint Shop Pro Photo X2, the process is similar. Click File > New and a New Image dialog box will open (see Figure 3.38). You can set the height, width, resolution, and type of background. For digital scrapbooking, you will want to choose a Raster Background in RGB 8-bit color depth.

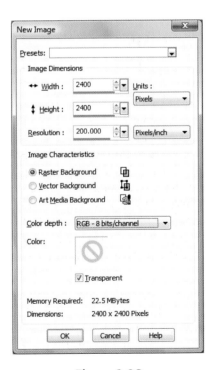

Figure 3.38

New Image dialog box in Paint Shop Pro Photo X2.

You can select either a transparent background or uncheck the Transparent check box and choose whatever color, pattern, or gradient that Paint Shop Pro Photo X2 contains in its Material Properties dialog (see Figure 3.39). This dialog box allows you to choose a background color for the image, as well as other colors for use in the application later, by clicking on the color swatch. If you choose a transparent background, you won't have to promote the Background layer to a regular layer later.

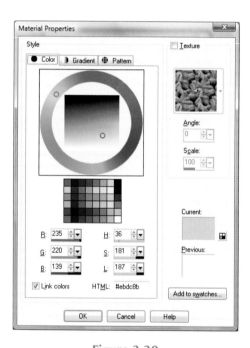

Figure 3.39

The Material Properties dialog box in Paint Shop Pro Photo X2.

Perhaps the easiest way to start a new layout is to open a background paper image that is already the size you want to create. Most scrapbook kits offer papers designed for 12×12- inch layouts, and some include 8.5×11-inch backgrounds as well. If one of those sizes meets your needs, just open a background paper image in your image editor, duplicate it or save a new copy so that you don't accidentally overwrite the original, and you are ready to begin.

Assembling the Layout

Once you've chosen and prepared your photos, chosen the scrapbook components you want to use, and determined the size of the layout, you are ready to assemble the elements.

Assembling a layout from separate components is much like creating a paper scrapbook page. Start with a background, add mats if desired, add photos, and then embellishments on top. If you paste in components as separate layers, you will be free to move those objects around the layout until you find a pleasing arrangement. Using the Layers palette in the image editor allows you to drag layers under or over each other, so if you find that an embellishment looks better partially hidden under another, just drag that layer beneath the object you want to appear on top.

Figure 3.40 shows a nearly-completed layout in Paint Shop Pro Photo X2. The scrapbook components shown in this layout are all included in the resources on the book's DVD. They include items from Doris Castle's Pink Magic kit, Lauren Bavin's Blossom Blush kit, Lie Fhung's Painting kit, and fonts from Kingthings Fonts. The components have all been pasted into the image on separate layers.

This allows us to move each item individually and to add effects to only the items we want to modify. If one object appears to be above another on the image, that's because it's actually higher in the Layers palette stack than the other object. We've also renamed the text layer to include the names of the fonts used, which will be handy if we need to modify the layout at a later date.

Figure 3.41 shows the Merge menu choices in Paint Shop Pro. Right-click on the layer title in the Layers palette, and choose Merge from the menu. The merge options are

- **Merge Down**—Merges the selected layer with the layer beneath it.

- **Merge All (Flatten)**—Merges all layers to a single Background layer.

- **Merge Visible**—Merges only those layers that are visible. To turn off layer visibility, click the visibility icon. Invisible layers will not be merged and may be made visible after the merge.

Figure 3.40

Layout assembled in Paint Shop Pro Photo X2. Layout elements by Lauren Bavin, Doris Castle, and Lie Fhung. Fonts are Kingthings, Printingkit, and Trypewriter.

Merging Layers

Layers are helpful features, but they do require the computer to work harder than with non-layered images. For this reason, it's best to *merge* layers with other layers as soon as you are sure no further modification to the objects on the layers will be needed. It's possible to merge only a few layers, leave others unmerged, or to merge them all. Once a layer is merged, the contents of that layer are locked in place with the other objects on that layer. The objects on a single layer can be moved in tandem, but not separately.

Figure 3.41

Layer Merge options in Paint Shop Pro Photo X2.

Photoshop Elements 5.0 has similar layer Merge options, as seen in Figure 3.42. You can also access the layer Merge options in the Layers Menu in the Menu toolbar in both Paint Shop Pro and Photoshop Elements.

Figure 3.42

Layer Merge options in Photoshop Elements 5.0.

It's a good idea to save a copy of the layout in progress with layers unmerged so that you can always return to it and modify it. But to work effectively, use a working copy of the layout and merge layers as you are satisfied with their positioning and scale.

Creating Realism

A few more basic techniques to learn, and you'll be on your way to creating beautiful albums quickly from Quick Pages and pre-made elements—creating realistic depth and shadows and "attaching" one object visually to another!

First—how to create the perception of depth in your layouts. You may notice that some elements come with shadows already created. These shadows are what make the embellishment appear to be sitting above the surface of the image. In reality, shadows are created when light emitted from a light source is blocked by a physical object. So if the sun is shining from the upper left of a scene, anything blocking the light will be shadowed to the lower right of the scene. Anything in the scene will be shadowed in the same direction—so when creating a faux paper layout, make sure all the shadows appear to be coming from the same light source.

To apply a shadow in Photoshop Elements 5.0, you can use a Layer Style, as you did earlier with text. Select the layer that contains the object you want to apply the shadow to by clicking on its layer title. In the Artwork and Effects palette, click on the Special Effects icon. Choose the Photo Effects category and Frames sub-category. Figure 3.43 shows the Special Effects tab with the Drop Shadows Low style. Click on the style icon to select it, and click Apply to apply the effect to the selected layer.

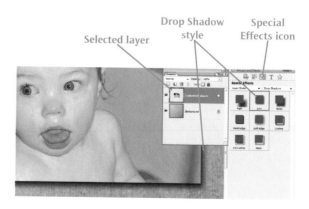

Figure 3.43

Special Effects tab in Photoshop Elements 5.0.

A copy of the original layer, with the style applied, will be created. If you'd like to modify the shadow effect, make sure the layer that has the style applied is selected, then go to Layers > Layer Style > Style Settings. A dialog box, as shown in Figure 3.44, will open and you can modify any of the style attributes. Click OK to apply the changes.

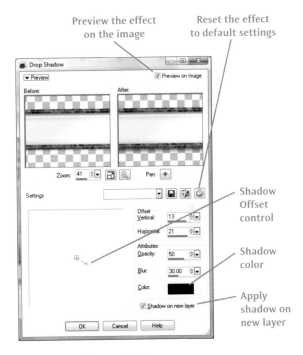

Preview the effect
on the image

Reset the effect
to default settings

Shadow
Offset
control

Shadow
color

Apply
shadow on
new layer

Figure 3.45

*Drop Shadow dialog in
Paint Shop Pro Photo X2.*

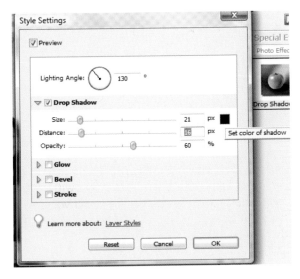

Set color of shadow

Figure 3.44

Style Settings dialog in Photoshop Elements 5.0.

Applying shadows in Paint Shop Pro is easy as well. Click on the layer title of the object you'd like to apply a shadow to, and go to Effects > 3D Effects > Drop Shadow. The dialog box shown in Figure 3.45 will open. Modify the direction of the shadow by typing in values in the Offset boxes or by dragging the center Offset control. Click on the control handle and drag in the direction you want the shadow applied.

Paint Shop Pro also allows you to preview the shadow directly on the image as you apply and modify it, as well as to create the shadow on its own layer, which allows you to modify the layer or remove it later. We've added a shadow to the nameplate and ribbon in the layout.

Another technique that helps create the illusion of realism in a faux paper layout is "attaching" one component to another, for example, attaching a charm to a ribbon or chain. This is accomplished by layering one object over the other, then selectively erasing an overlapping section.

Open, copy, and paste the element you want to attach into the layout. In Figure 3.46 you can see that we've added a heart charm to the layout and moved it into position above the safety pin on the nameplate.

The tool that you'll use for this task is the Eraser Tool. Both Paint Shop Pro and Photoshop Elements have an Eraser Tool, found on the toolbar. Click on the tool's icon to activate it. In Figures 3.47 and 3.48, you can see the Tool Options for the Eraser Tool in both applications.

Set the Eraser size to be small enough to erase just inside the width of the charm's link. In this case, that value is 9–10 pixels. Click on the heart charm's layer title in the Layers palette to make sure that layer is selected, and zoom in if necessary to work on the link detail. Carefully erase the portion of the link that lies over the bottom pin's spring so that the charm link appears to pass through the spring, as in Figure 3.49.

Figure 3.46

Charm image pasted above nameplate layer.

Figure 3.47

Eraser Tool options in Photoshop Elements 5.0.

Figure 3.48

Eraser Tool options in Paint Shop Pro Photo X2.

Erase link on top layer

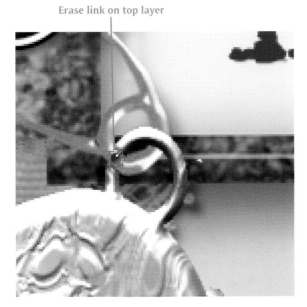

Figure 3.49

Charm link detail erased.

Add a drop shadow to the heart charm to make it appear higher off the page than the objects beneath it. If the drop shadow style you are using allows you to modify blur, softness or offset values, try varying those to achieve softer shadow effects. Once you're satisfied with all the details, save your image, and your layout is complete! (See Figure 3.50.)

Figure 3.50

Completed layout, with elements by Lauren Bavin, Doris Castle, Lie Fhung, and Sally Beacham.

Calendar pages by Sally Beacham, with photos by Ron Lacey and components from the Universal Calendar kit by Lie Fhung, available on this book's resource DVD.

4

Hybrid Scrapbooking

ICTURE YOURSELF CREATING BEAUTIFUL and useful objects using your new skills and scrapbook resources. Imagine combining your digital images with craft supplies to create printable projects like greeting cards, calendars, gift boxes, and albums of every imaginable type. That's what hybrid scrapbooking is all about—combining digital techniques with paper products to create all sorts of projects.

Hybrid Scrapbooking—What Is It?

SIMPLY PUT, HYBRID scrapbooking is combining digital and paper components to create printable projects. Decorated CD cases (and albums inside), greeting cards, invitations, party decorations, calendars, gift boxes, gift wrap, or bags—if it's a paper craft, you can use your digital supplies to create it! (See Figure 4.1.)

Figure 4.1

Decorative box, using elements from Doris Castle's Heritage Legacy kit, by Denise Doupnik.

One advantage of using digital files in these projects is that you'll always have a re-usable image that you can print multiple times (unlike paper crafting supplies, which must be replaced). As you'll learn in Chapter 11, "Inspiration," you can always have digital supplies that match your chosen color scheme, and you can even make your own papers and elements to coordinate exactly with your project.

If you've done traditional paper scrapbooking, you probably have lots of supplies you can incorporate into your creations. If you're new to scrapbooking of any type, you'll find the following supplies handy:

- Cutting tools, such as scissors or a paper trimmer

- Adhesives, which should be marked "acid- and lignin-free"

- Preservatives to prevent smudging or water-spotting of inkjet prints

- Decorative objects to add to your projects

Using Digital Elements in Paper Projects

That's exactly what you can do—print out digital elements, cut them out, and adhere them to traditional paper layouts, much like you would add a purchased sticker. If you've printed the digital components on an inkjet printer, they won't be water-resistant. If you want to use them in a project that won't be covered by a protective sleeve, you can use a spray-on fixative, found at art or craft stores, which can improve the paper's water-resistance.

You can also laminate the element after you print and cut it out. Hot laminating machines designed for hobby use come in several sizes and are fairly inexpensive. You will need special hot laminating pouches to use in this type of machine. Cold lamination sheets don't require special equipment. Once the item is laminated, trim it so that only a small edge of clear plastic material is visible, and then adhere it to your project.

Background papers are printed so easily from digital files! You can print as many copies as you like and never have to worry about running out of that special pattern you've been using throughout an entire album. You can colorize papers to match any layout, too. And if you don't have a printer capable of printing 12×12-inch paper, some standard printers have a banner print setting that allows you to split a large image across several sheets that can then be adhered together to produce a larger print. There are also software applications that can help, such as ProPoster at www.ronyasoft.com/products/proposter/.

Glue, Glue, Who's Got the Glue?

There are so many choices for scrapbooking adhesives, and to cover them all might require a book of its own! Fortunately, as a digital scrapbooker you don't have to worry about the archival properties of adhesives, which can limit the choices of a traditional scrapbooker. But the sheer variety of adhesives can be mind-boggling. There are glue sticks, glue dots, glue squares, tape-runners, and adhesive applicators and tapes of every description. Adhesives are also available as permanent or re-positionable. Re-positionable adhesives don't bond immediately, so you can move the scrapbook component to a different spot if you like. Another useful type of adhesive is foam tape of varying thickness—this can be used to lift the element off the page for a dimensional look.

Be sure to check the adhesive to make sure it's appropriate for use with your project components. Bleed-through of liquid adhesive to the front of the printed image is common, and it will ruin the look of your image. You may need to use special paper to prevent this.

Hybrid Projects

T HE TYPES OF CRAFT PROJECTS you
can create from digital files are limited only
by your imagination. You'll need some basic
craft supplies, which can be obtained at craft stores,
art or office supply stores, or discount stores. Even
common household objects can be pressed into
service! Some software applications include templates or special features to help create popular
projects.

Greeting Cards

Personalized greeting cards and invitations are
popular paper craft items. Traditional paper
crafters often use scrapbook supplies and techniques to create greeting cards. In particular, rubber stamping is a popular technique that can be
used for all types of paper crafts. Figure 4.2 shows
a paper greeting card created with rubber stamps
from Lie Fhung's Ztampf! line of stamps. Fhung
also creates digital scrapbook files, many of which
can be found on this book's DVD. Figure 4.3 shows
a variety of paper supplies that were used to create
those cards. Beautiful, but once you use them,
they're gone. With digital files, you'll always have a
ready supply of renewable, printable papers and
embellishments.

Figure 4.2

*Greeting cards using rubber stamps from Ztampf!
by Lie Fhung, created by Norene Malaney.*

Figure 4.3

Paper supplies used to create greeting cards.

Card Creator Applications?

There are a number of dedicated paper crafting applications on the market. They are easy to use and often include lots of clipart and fonts. However, they may not allow you to import your own images or save your creations as digital files that could be used in other applications. For that reason, we're going to create our projects in the image editors we've been using in this book, Adobe Photoshop Elements and Corel Paint Shop Pro Photo X2.

You can easily create all-digital images to be printed as greeting cards using your scrapbook resources. Figure 4.4 shows a greeting card created in Paint Shop Pro Photo X2 with scrapbook components from Lie Fhung, which can be found on this book's DVD. Can you tell the "real" card from its digital cousin, in Figure 4.5?

Figure 4.4

Digital greeting card using scrapbook components from Ztampf! by Lie Fhung, created by Sally Beacham.

Figure 4.5

Which is the "real" card?

You'll want to create your greeting card image with the dimensions of the printed card in mind. Avery and other manufactures make pre-scored greeting card stock in standard paper sizes. Avery has printing templates available at www.avery.com for Microsoft Word and Adobe image editors that are very easy to use, and Paint Shop Pro Photo X2 has several templates built-in to its Print Layout feature, including some Avery templates.

Photoshop Elements has a Greeting Card project available in its Create options, but the layout is not designed to be printed as a folded greeting card, but rather as a post card. To access the Create menu:

- In Photoshop Elements 5.0, go to File > Create > Greeting Card, or click the Create button in the main toolbar (see Figure 4.6).

- In Photoshop Elements 6.0, click the Create tab on the workspace, choose More Options, and then Greeting Card (see Figure 4.7).

Figure 4.6

Greeting Card option in Photoshop Elements 5.0.

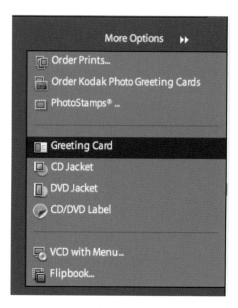

Figure 4.7

Greeting Card option in Photoshop Elements 6.0.

What Else Can I Make?

Photoshop Elements 5.0 and 6.0 have built-in options for creating other printable projects, too. The Photo Layout option will create a 12×12-inch or 8.5×11-inch scrapbook page. There are also projects for photo books, photo calendars, and photo stamps (yes, your own custom postage!), which can be uploaded directly to Adobe's own online printing site. You can also create CD or DVD labels and jackets or build a slide-show or online gallery. In Elements 6.0, you can also burn a VCD that can be viewed on any CD or DVD player.

When the Greeting Card dialog is open, you'll see options for card size, number of photos, and an optional theme. Choose No Theme if you'd like to use your own background images, or use one of the pre-made background themes. Figure 4.8 shows the New Greeting Card dialog in Photoshop Elements 5.0.

The Simple Frame themes add Polaroid-type frames around your chosen images, and they are resizable. Press OK to create the postcard template.

Once the template is created, switch to the Edit mode, click on a photo frame to add a photo from your hard drive, or drag an image that is already open in the workspace and drop it on the selected frame (make sure you switch to the Mover tool to do this). The image will be automatically resized to fit the frame. You can rotate the image in the frame, rotate the frame and image together, and re-position the framed image to better suit the card layout.

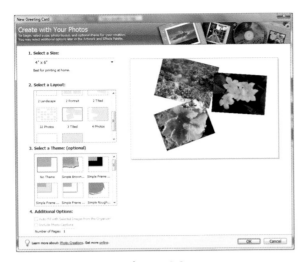

Figure 4.8

Greeting Card option in Photoshop Elements 5.0.

If you'd like to modify the scale of the image within the frame, use the slider control to zoom the image in or out in the frame. You can also use the Fit Frame to Photo option by right-clicking on the image. The frame will be re-sized and re-oriented to match the aspect ratio of the photo you're using (see Figure 4.9).

Figure 4.9

Place photos with Fit Frame to Photo option in Photoshop Elements 5.0.

You can add your own background image in a layer above the background layer. Highlight the background layer in the Layers palette, then go to File > Place. Browse to find the background image or digital paper of your choice, and click OK. A new layer is created, and the image will be placed on it. However, it will be scaled to fit within the postcard template and may not completely cover the background layer. Grab a corner handle and drag the digital paper out large enough to cover the postcard's background layer. Figure 4.10 shows the new background pattern layer added above the background layer in the Layers palette.

Figure 4.10

Layers palette in Photoshop Elements 5.0, with background image added.

Add scrapbook components of your choice and text. Figure 4.11 shows a postcard image with digital elements from the book's DVD added, as well as some text. Your custom-made postcard is ready to print!

Figure 4.11

Finished postcard ready to print.

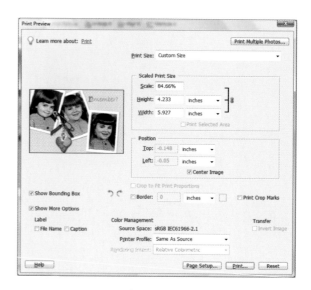

Figure 4.12

Print Preview dialog in Photoshop Elements 5.0

Go to File > Print to access the Print Preview dialog. Click the Page Setup button to choose the paper type you'll be printing. Set the height and width values in the Scaled Print Size section. If the preview panel shows that the image is not scaled to your liking, modify the values by changing the Scale percentage until you are satisfied. You can also change the scale and position of the image by unchecking the Center Image option, and then dragging the image in the preview panel.

Check the Print Crop Marks option if you'd like to print the postcard on a larger sheet of paper and then trim it down to the finished size. (See Figure 4.12.)

Paint Shop Pro Photo X2 doesn't have a dedicated greeting card maker. However, it *does* have a Print Layout feature that uses pre-made card templates (and allows you to create custom templates, too) that can make half-fold and quarter-fold cards.

Create separate images for each side of the card that you'd like to print. You'll need one image for the front, one for any text that should be printed inside the card, and perhaps a third image for the back of the card. It's helpful to have these images open on the Paint Shop Pro workspace, although you can also browse to a file from within the Print Layout dialog.

Go to File > Print Layout. When the Print Layout dialog opens, click on File > Open Template. As shown in Figure 4.13, there are several categories of templates available, including many templates designed to work with Avery brand paper products.

Description of paper type   Click on template icon

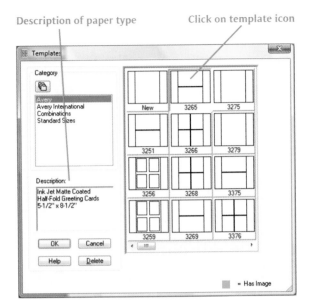

Figure 4.13

Print Layout template dialog in Paint Shop Pro Photo X2

You will notice that the card images are created in portrait aspect mode. The card template is designed in landscape orientation, but no worries! Rotate the front image by clicking the Rotate Right icon in the toolbar. The image will be resized to fit the cell as it is rotated to the proper position.

Drag image to template cell   Rotate image in cell by using Rotate Right or Rotate Left buttons

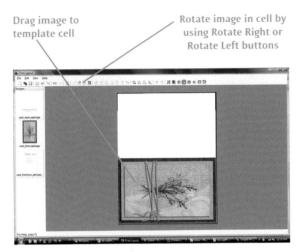

Figure 4.14

Greeting card image positioned in card template.

Choose a card template that works with your paper choice. The 5 1/2 × 8 1/2-inch card templates can also be used with standard card stock—just fold the paper in half! Click OK, and the template is created in the open Print Layout workspace. The images you previously created and left open in the main application workspace are shown as thumbnail images on the left side of the Layout dialog. Drag an image to the appropriate position in the template, and drop it in the cell. In Figure 4.14, the front of the card image has been dropped in the bottom cell of the card template. When the card is printed and folded, the image will show on the front of the card only.

If you want to use an image for the back of the card, drag it to the top cell of the template. In this case, the image should be printed at the bottom of the back side of the folded card, so it should be rotated to the right once. If you are creating a card that will be folded in landscape orientation, rotate the top cell image so that it reads upside-down on the template. It will then be in proper position when the card is folded, as shown in Figure 4.15. Click and drag on the image to position it where you like in the top cell.

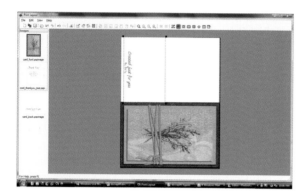

Figure 4.15

Greeting card images rotated and positioned in the card template.

To print text on the inside of the card, you will probably need to print the first side, remove the card from the printer and re-position it to be printed on the second side (unless you have a printer capable of two-sided printing). Use the same template to create the print layout for the second side, and place the text image in the bottom cell of the template. (See Figure 4.16). Reprint the card, fold it, sign it, and you're finished!

Heads or Tails?

It's a good idea to print a test copy on scrap paper to check what orientation your printer uses for a double-sided print. Some printers use face-up, head-first paper orientation, and others use face-down, head-last orientation. You should be certain that the paper is fed in the proper orientation to place the images on the second side correctly. You won't want to ruin a great card by printing the second side upside-down!

Figure 4.16

Greeting card template with text image positioned.

Calendars

Some of the most popular hybrid scrapbooking projects are custom calendars, featuring your own photos and scrapbook layouts. Calendars make terrific gifts, and since you can create one calendar and print it multiple times, they are great time-savers, too!

Online Websites like Shutterfly and Snapfish have easy calendar options—just upload the layouts you want to use and follow their wizards to create the calendar of your choice. These sites are usually designed to accept an 8.5×11-inch layout as the image section of the calendar. A 12-month calendar will cost about $20 US. Some sites also allow you to create 18-month calendars or calendars of different sizes. Make sure that the layouts you choose will be proportioned to your liking in the calendar wizard.

If you don't want to order online, office supply stores and local photo developers will also create custom calendars for you for comparable pricing. Calendars are usually wire-ring bound, and you should choose a special layout as the cover image for a nice presentation.

You can also create your own calendars and print them at home. For about $10 US, you can buy a inkjet calendar printing kit, such as the one shown in Figure 4.17 from Strathmore Artist Papers. This kit can be found at office supply stores, art stores, and online retailers. It includes double-sided pre-punched calendar pages and a binding system that requires no special tools.

Figure 4.17

Strathmore inkjet calendar kit.

The pages in the kit are 8.5×11 inches, but they are designed with a half-inch border around the layout image, so you'll need a finished image of 7.5×10 inches. You can use square layouts if you like—just resize them to 7.5 inches square and add some additional patterned paper on either side (or leave it plain).

73

Sometimes the hardest part of creating your own calendar is to create the monthly grid with appropriate dates! But there's a great solution included on this book's DVD—a universal calendar creator kit from Lie Fhung. The folder containing the kit can be found in the resource section, and it is titled ZtampCalendar_UniversalTemplates_200dpi. The kit includes instructions for creating a calendar for any year and pre-made grid templates for each month, as well as some decorative elements to highlight holidays and special events, as seen in Figure 4.18.

You can create a traditional two-page per month calendar by printing a layout on the top page of the calendar and using the calendar kit's grid images for the bottom page. Extra numbers are included for months with 31 days. For that special month with only 28 (occasionally 29!) days, just delete the extra days from the grid on the template you use.

Another type of calendar uses a single page per month, and it uses a layout or photo as a background image with a calendar grid incorporated as part of the layout. Figure 4.19 shows the Ztampf! kit used in this manner. Add text and your favorite digital elements to complete the calendar and personalize it.

Block Background   Clear Background   INSTRUCTIONS.rtf   Ztampf_ReadMe...   Ztampf_SaveYou...   ZtampfCalendar...   ZtampfCalendar...

31 **31** **31** ○ □ ♡

ZtampfCalendar...   ZtampfCalendar...   ZtampfCalendar...   ZtampfCalendar...   ZtampfCalendar...   ZtampfCalendar...   ZtampfCalendar_...

Figure 4.18

Contents of Lie Fhung's Ztampf! Universal Calendar template kit found on the book's DVD.

Figure 4.19

Sample calendar page by Lie Fhung for Ztampf!

Many scrapbook designers make calendar kits, some in smaller sizes that are designed to fit frames that can be found at craft stores. Visit a local shop and see what's available—you're sure to find something that can be used to create a personalized custom calendar that is your own unique creation.

Printing Kits

Strathmore Artist Papers makes a couple other kits that the digital scrapbooker might find useful. Photo Album kits in two sizes (8×8 inches and 8.5×11 inches) are available. The kits include 20 double-sided sheets of pre-punched photo paper, post binding hardware, and sturdy black polyvinyl covers. The cost is approximately $10-12 US per kit. This makes an economical album, since a single standard album will cost that much without photo paper.

Other Projects

Decorative objects such as gift boxes, candy bar wrappers for party favors, and specialty albums are just a few projects that can be created using digital scrapbook images. Figure 4.1 at the beginning of this chapter shows a beautiful gift box created by Denise Doupnik with digital images by Doris Castle, which can be found on this book's DVD. Adding traditional scrapbook embellishments along with digital images makes for a beautiful and unique project.

Accordion-fold albums are very easy to create—just print out layouts in the proper size to fit the album and adhere. Figure 4.20 shows just such an album. This album folds flat for storage, but stands for display as well.

Figure 4.20

Accordion album by Lauren Bavin.

Miniature albums are great gifts and easy to carry in purse or pocket. Figure 4.21 shows a laminated mini-album. This type of album could also be strung on a keychain or tied with ribbon. Notice that the layouts are laminated to protect them from wear and tear?

Figure 4.21

Laminated mini-album by Lauren Bavin.

Figure 4.22

Block album and tray by Lauren Bavin.

Another unusual album type is a wooden block album. This consists of a set of wooden or cardboard blocks, with layout images adhered to the sides, and often placed in a matching decorative tray. Be sure to use adhesive that is intended for use with wood and paper, and check for bleed-through so that the printed images aren't damaged by the process. Figure 4.22 shows a block album and tray.

Hybrid scrapbooking projects are limited only by your imagination. If you can make it with paper, you can use your digital files to create it.

Part II
It's All About the Photos

Sunset on the Bay

Stone Harbor
New Jersey
August 12, 2006

Photograph
by
Nicole D'Achille

"Sunset" layout by Roberta D'Achille. Photo by Nicole D'Achille.

Tools
of my trade

✓ camera
✓ scanner
✓ pinter
✓ Memories!

2007

"Tools of My Trade" layout by Sally Beacham, components by Doris Castle and Roberta D'Achille, photos by Ron Lacey.

Handling the Hardware

PICTURE YOURSELF IN YOUR OWN scrapbooking studio. In addition to your computer, you have a digital camera and photo printer, and maybe even a scanner and a graphics tablet. You're ready to capture some memories, convert your old photos to digital images, and then print those lovely photos and the scrapbook layouts you create. In this chapter, we'll examine some of the hardware you'll need to make your digital scrapbook studio a reality.

Digital Camera Basics

THESE DAYS DIGITAL CAMERAS are so affordable that they are within easy reach of almost any computer user. In fact, many computer manufacturers bundle digital cameras with their entry-level home computers. However, the quality of the photos you get will depend on your camera. Some of the bundled cameras might be fine for producing photos for display on Web pages, but not quite what you'd want for anything but the smallest of print images. Let's review some of the basics of digital cameras to be sure that the camera you use is right for the job.

Resolution: Megapixels and You

If you know nothing else about digital cameras, you probably know that *megapixels* (MP) have something to do with the quality of the photos a digital camera produces. What are megapixels and why are they important? *Pixels* are the basic blocks of color that make up a digital image, and megapixels are the millions of pixels that a camera can capture. Figure 5.1 shows a magnified portion of a digital photo, revealing the blocks of color that are pixels.

The number of megapixels a camera can capture is usually referred to as the camera's *resolution*. Resolution is one of the major factors that determine the quality of the photo and how it can be used. Other factors include the type of light sensor used in your camera, the quality of the camera's lens, and the amount and kind of compression, if any, that your camera applies to captured images.

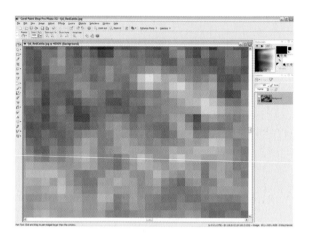

Figure 5.1

Pixels are the basic blocks of color that make up a digital image.

Early digital cameras had resolutions of only 1 MP or 2 MP. Nearly all of today's cameras have resolutions of 6 MP or more. For printed photos and scrapbook pages, you'll probably want a camera with a resolution of at least 5 MP, which is fine for 8×10-inch photo prints or even larger.

Focus

All digital cameras include automatic focus. This suits most purposes, although sometimes you'll want to have more control over what areas of your photo are in sharp focus and what areas are not. For example, you may be shooting a photo of a person who happens to be standing several feet in front of a building that occupies the center of your composition. In this case, you want to be sure that it's the person and not the building that's in focus. Since the automatic focus targets the center of your photo, you could have a problem here, as shown in Figure 5.2. You can avoid this problem by using your camera's manual focus control, if there is one.

Figure 5.2

Automatic focus might target something other than the subject of your photo.

Focus Lock

There is a way around the person-in-front-of-the-building problem, even if your camera has only automatic focus. Nearly all digital cameras let you lock the focus by pressing the shutter release button only halfway down, not actually taking the photo until you press the button all the way down. To use focus lock, center the focus target over the object you want in focus, press the shutter release button halfway down and hold it. Then compose your photo as you like and press the shutter release all the way down to take the shot.

Exposure

Cameras produce photos by capturing light. The amount of light that enters the camera is the *exposure*. By controlling the exposure, you control which areas of the photo show detail, whether areas of motion are frozen or blurred, and how much of the photo is in sharp focus. If you let in too little light, your photo will be underexposed, making the image overly dark and obscuring detail in the shadow areas, as illustrated in Figure 5.3. If you let in too much light, your photo will be overexposed, washing out the image's colors and eliminating detail in the highlight areas, as illustrated in Figure 5.4.

Figure 5.4

Overexposure eliminates detail in the highlights.

Figure 5.3

Underexposure obscures details in the shadows.

Figure 5.5

A long shutter speed blurs motion.

Two things control exposure: *shutter speed* and *aperture*. Shutter speed controls the length of time that light is allowed to enter the camera. Aperture controls how large the opening is that lets in the light. Longer shutter speeds blur areas of motion (see Figure 5.5), while shorter shutter speeds freeze areas of motion (see Figure 5.6).

Figure 5.6

A short shutter speed freezes motion.

Figure 5.7

Large apertures produce a shallow depth of field.

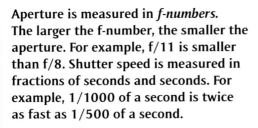

Measurement of Aperture
and Shutter Speed

**Aperture is measured in *f-numbers*.
The larger the f-number, the smaller the
aperture. For example, f/11 is smaller
than f/8. Shutter speed is measured in
fractions of seconds and seconds. For
example, 1/1000 of a second is twice
as fast as 1/500 of a second.**

Figure 5.8

Smaller apertures increase the depth of field .

The area of sharp focus in a photo is called *depth of field*. Larger apertures reduce the depth of field (see Figure 5.7), keeping only a shallow area in focus and blurring areas that are closer to the camera and farther away from the camera than the subject you're focusing on. Smaller apertures increase the depth of field (see Figure 5.8), keeping a deeper area in focus.

Cameras and Lenses

Early digital cameras had only unremovable fixed-focus lenses, which were fine for snapshots of landscapes and group portraits, but not so good for portraits of individuals or for close-ups. Nearly all digital cameras today come with zoom lenses, enabling you to change the focal length of the lens as it suits the situation, from wide-angle to telephoto.

Compact digital cameras have a single lens that is permanently attached to the camera. The lens on today's compact digital cameras is a zoom lens, which enables you to adjust the focal length to suit your needs. The range of focal lengths, called the *zoom factor*, can be anywhere from 3X (three levels of magnification) to 10X or more.

All digital cameras have automatic exposure controls, and in many cases that's sufficient. If you want to have more control over exposure, you'll want a camera with semi-automatic exposure controls or even manual exposure controls. Here are the possibilities:

- ⊙ **Fully automatic.** The camera determines both the shutter speed and aperture.

- ⊙ **Aperture priority.** You set the aperture and the camera chooses an appropriate shutter speed, enabling you to control depth of field.

- ⊙ **Shutter priority.** You set the shutter speed and the camera chooses an appropriate aperture, enabling you to freeze motion or blur areas of motion.

- ⊙ **Manual.** You control both the aperture and shutter speed.

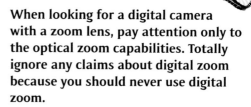

Prosumer digital cameras are a step up from compact digital cameras. They have somewhat larger sensors, a greater distance between the lens and the sensor, and larger lenses. The camera body is larger and a bit heftier than compact cameras, which means you may be better able to hold them steady. These cameras usually also have lenses that accommodate photographic filters, such as polarizers.

Lens Converters

Some prosumer digital cameras have lens converters for ultra wide-angle or long telephoto shots, significantly expanding the usability of the camera.

Figure 5.9 shows an example of a typical prosumer camera compared with a typical compact camera.

Figure 5.9

Typical prosumer camera (left) and typical compact camera (right).

If your digital camera budget allows it, you might even consider a *digital SLR*, which has a camera body much like a 35mm film camera and removable, interchangeable lenses, as shown in Figure 5.10. These cameras produce high-quality photos, and although the prices are relatively steep, these high performance cameras are becoming more and more affordable every day.

Figure 5.10

A digital SLR resembles a 35mm film camera and has interchangeable lenses.

A digital SLR offers many advantages over a compact digital or a prosumer camera. The larger sensor of a digital SLR provides a wide range for depth of field and also eliminates the dreaded shutter lag common to compact cameras and, to a lesser extent, prosumer cameras. (*Shutter lag* is the gap between the time you press the camera's shutter release and the time the camera actually captures the image—something that can be quite frustrating if your subject is a moving target, such as a small child or a pet.) Digital SLRs also have the advantage of allowing you to use whatever lens is best for the particular situation: a wide-angle for your landscape shots, short telephoto for portraits, and long telephoto for frame-filling wildlife or sports shots.

Focal Length Multiplier

Because a digital SLR's sensor is smaller than the focal area of a 35mm film camera, a lens designed for a 35mm camera will have a greater effective focal length when used on a digital SLR. Typically, you'd multiply the focal length of the lens by 1.5 to get the effective focal length on the digital SLR. So, for example, a 200mm lens that is designed for use on a film camera but is used on a digital SLR will give you the same result as a 300mm lens on a film camera. This can be a big boon when you're doing telephoto work, but it can be a limitation when what you need is a wide-angle shot. For example, on a digital SLR, a 28mm lens designed for a film camera may behave like a 42mm lens when used on a digital SLR.

For more information on the various digital camera options, visit www.dpreview.com. You'll find in-depth reviews and comparisons of various cameras, as well as glossaries of camera-related terms and user forums for many camera brands.

Memory and Power Sources

Although your digital camera doesn't use any film, it does need a place to store images. There are several kinds of storage for digital cameras, and different brands and models of cameras use different kinds of storage. Some common storage media types are CompactFlash cards, SD cards, and xD-Picture Cards. Figure 5.11 shows some examples of memory cards.

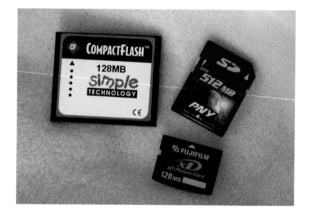

Figure 5.11

A few types of memory cards.

Be sure to get the right kind of memory media for your camera—and plenty of it. You don't want to run out of storage space far from your computer right in the middle of an important event that you'd like to record.

Memory Card Capacity

In the past, memory cards held relatively little data—64MB or less. Since a high quality photo image can take up about 2MB or more, it isn't surprising that card capacity is now much higher than 64MB. Today, a typical card capacity is 1GB, 2GB, or even more.

You'll also need batteries for your camera. Use rechargeables if your camera accepts them, and keep some spare batteries on hand. You don't want to have your batteries die just as you're about to take an important shot.

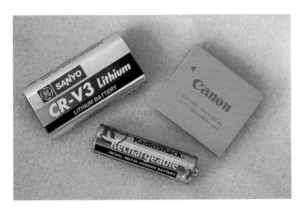

Figure 5.12

Different types of batteries used in digital cameras.

In addition to batteries, you'll probably want an AC adapter for your camera. You can use the adapter when you're offloading your photos to your computer. That way, you'll save your batteries for when you really need them. You can also use the adapter as your power source for indoor shots such as portraits or still lifes.

Battery Charging

To prolong their life, rechargeable NiCad and NiMH batteries need to be fully discharged before recharging. If your camera uses one of these types of batteries, get a charger that includes a discharge function, and discharge your batteries before charging them again. You can find these chargers at many sources, such as your local camera shop or online photo supply store.

Unlike NiCad and NiMH batteries, rechargeable Li-ion batteries do not need to be fully discharged before being charged (and in fact should not be discharged).

Other Considerations

This information just touches on what's involved in digital photography. Be sure to check your camera's documentation for other topics, such as white balance, different types of metering, and any special features that are available on your camera. If you don't yet have a camera, check out the Web sites of different manufacturers, such as Canon, Epson, Fujifilm, HP, Kodak, Minolta, Nikon, Olympus, Pentax, and Sony. And as we mentioned earlier, also take a look at the reviews and useful content at Digital Photography Review (www.dpreview.com).

Card Readers

Most computers these days include a memory card reader, and there are also portable card readers that you can plug into your computer. If you have a card reader, you don't need to have your camera on to get your photos onto your computer. Instead, remove the card from the camera, pop it into the appropriate slot in your card reader, and copy your photo files directly from the card.

Scanning Basics

IF ALL OF YOUR PHOTOS are taken with a digital camera, then it's a simple matter to save your photos to your computer using either the camera's software, the operating system's media support, or image editing software. However, if you have physical photo prints or slides, you'll need to scan your photos in order to get digital versions. Most copying services can scan your photos for you. You can also scan the photos yourself using a desktop flatbed scanner (see Figure 5.13).

There are quite a few good personal scanners available from manufacturers such as Epson, Canon, and HP. For photo scanning, you'll want one with an optical resolution of at least 600 dots per inch (dpi)—2,400 dpi or 4,800 dpi preferred—and at least 24-bit color depth. If you want to scan slides or negatives, be sure the scanner includes a transparency adapter. At the time of writing this book, a good 4,800 dpi scanner with transparency adapter could be purchased for as little as US$150.

Figure 5.13

You can scan your film photos at home with a flatbed scanner.

Dedicated Film Scanners

If you have boxes and boxes of negatives or slides to scan, you may want to consider a dedicated film scanner like the one shown in Figure 5.14. Be aware, however, that dedicated scanners are fairly expensive, with a good one easily running in the range of US$750–$1,000.

Figure 5.14

A dedicated film scanner. (Photo by Ron Lacey)

You can scan 3D objects as well as photos. Shirt buttons, door keys, and other objects can be scanned to use as scrapbook elements in your digital layouts. Just lift up the scanner cover or remove it completely, place the objects on the scanner bed, drape a cloth over the objects to cover the scanner bed, and then scan as you normally would. Some scanners even have an adjustable lid that accommodates small objects for scanning. If what you want to scan is liquid or something like oatmeal or sand, place the material in a transparent container such as a Pyrex dish, as shown in Figure 5.15.

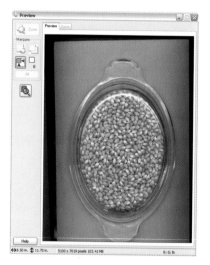

Figure 5.16

Preview of some popcorn about to be scanned.

Figure 5.15

You can scan liquids and granular materials in a transparent dish placed on a flatbed scanner.

Figure 5.16 shows a scanner's preview of some popcorn that's about to be scanned in this way, and Figure 5.17 shows the resulting scanned image in Paint Shop Pro Photo.

Figure 5.17

The scanned popcorn in Paint Shop Pro Photo.

Scanning Resolution

One of the most basic, but sometimes confusing, scanning topics is resolution. When speaking of scanning, resolution doesn't refer to the total number of pixels or megapixels like digital camera resolution. Instead, *scanner resolution* refers to the number of samples per inch or dots per inch that the scanner reads.

The easiest way to approach scanner resolution is to look at a real example. Suppose you have an 8×10-inch photo that you want to scan. If you scan this photo at 200 dpi (that is, 200 dots per inch), you'll get a digital image that's 200 dpi × 8 inches by 200 dpi × 10 inches—1,600 pixels by 2,000 pixels. (Each dot or sample scanned yields one pixel in your digital image.) If you scanned the same image at 400 dpi, you'd get an image that's 400 dpi × 8 inches by 400 dpi × 10 inches—3,200 pixels by 4000 pixels. If each of these scans were printed with an image resolution of 200 pixels per inch (ppi), you'd get an 8×10-inch print in the first case and a 16×20-inch print in the second case.

File Size and Scan Resolution

In the example, the 400 dpi scan would take up four times as much space on your hard drive as the 200 dpi scan because the 400 dpi version is both twice as high and twice as wide as the 200 dpi version.

DPI and PPI

If you're confused about DPI and PPI, you're far from alone. One thing that adds to the confusion is that DPI (dots per inch) is used to refer to three very different things: scanning resolution, printer resolution, and image resolution.

For scanning resolution, DPI represents the number of pixels that you get in your scanned image for each inch of the physical thing you scan.

For printer resolution, DPI represents the number of dots of ink that the printer applies for every inch of a print it makes. The number of dots in the print doesn't correspond one to one with the number of pixels in the image you're printing: multiple dots of ink are applied for each pixel in your image. When you make a print, you probably won't set the printer resolution in terms of DPI directly, but rather you'll find settings such as Photo Quality and Enhanced Photo Quality.

For image resolution, DPI is more properly called PPI (pixels per inch). Image resolution is an instruction to your printer, telling the printer how close together it should print the pixels in your image. Increase the PPI, and you'll get a smaller print because the pixels in your image will be packed more tightly together than they would be with a smaller PPI.

A Few Scanning Tips

When you scan your photos, follow these bits of advice:

- **Choose the settings appropriate for what you're scanning**. Prints should be scanned using your scanner's full color or grayscale settings (full color for color photos and either full color or grayscale for black and white). Negatives and slides should be scanned with transparency settings, if available, and you may also need to tell your scanner whether the transparency you're scanning is a negative.

- **Choose the appropriate resolution.** If you'll print your photos at an image resolution of 200 ppi, then scan at 200 dpi to get a print that's the same size as the physical photo. If you want to print at a larger size than the original, increase the scan resolution in order to get a larger number of pixels. For example, to print a 4×5-inch original at 8×10 inches with an image resolution of 200 ppi, set the scan resolution to 400 dpi. Your scanned image will then be 1,600 pixels × 2,000 pixels, just what you need for an 8×10-inch print of a 200 ppi image.

- **If you're interested in only part of the original, scan only that part**. Virtually all scanners have a means of restricting the scan to a portion of the original. You might want that smaller portion to print at larger than its original size, so in that case remember to increase the scan resolution to get all the pixels you need to make a larger print.

For a lot more information on scanning, head over to Wayne Fulton's Scan Tips at www.scantips.com.

Choosing a Photo Printer

A NY GOOD PHOTO-QUALITY inkjet printer can be used to print your layouts. Perhaps the most popular models among scrappers are those from Canon, Epson, and HP. Any photo-quality printer can print layouts up to 8×10 inches (and even up to 8.5×11 inches if the printer can produce full-bleed borderless prints). However, if you want to print your 12×12-inch layouts at home, you'll need a wide-format printer.

Good photo-quality printers can be purchased for about US$100 to $300. Wide-format printers, like the one shown in Figure 5.18, can be considerably more expensive. Table 5.1 lists a few of the wide-format printers available.

Figure 5.18

A wide-format printer accommodates 12×12-inch layouts. (Photo by Ron Lacey)

Table 5.1 Wide-format photo-quality inkjet printers

Manufacturer	Model	Price (US$)
Canon	PIXMA Pro9000	499.99
Canon	PIXMA Pro9500	849.99
Epson	Stylus Photo R1400	399.99
Epson	Stylus Photo R1800	549.00
Epson	Stylus Photo R2400	849.99
HP	Photosmart Pro B8350 Photo	349.99
HP	Photosmart 8750 Professional	499.99
HP	Photosmart Pro B9180 Photo	699.99

Photo-quality printers use one of two types of ink: dye-based and pigment-based. Until recently, dye-based inks generally had the widest color ranges, but pigment-based inks have recently been catching up. Pigment-based inks generally produce the most water-resistant and fade-resistant prints, with some pigment-based inks purported to produce prints that last without fading for over 100 years when used with the manufacturer's recommended paper. When choosing your printer, be sure to check what type of ink it uses. Select a model that uses the sort of ink that has the characteristics that are most important to you.

Shades of Gray

Some printers have the option of using *photo gray* or *light black* ink in addition to standard black ink. This option might be important to you if you do a lot of black-and-white photo printing.

What printer is right for you? When you go shopping for a printer, here are some things to keep in mind:

- **Do you design your layouts larger than 8.5×11 inches?** If so, you need a wide-format printer. If not, you'll probably want to stick with a standard photo-quality model, which will almost certainly cost less than a comparable wide-format model.

- **Is maximum water-resistance and fade-resistance important to you?** If so, choose a printer that uses pigment-based inks. Pigment-based inks can

produce prints that, when printed on the proper paper and stored under proper conditions, should show no noticeable fading for 100 years or more. Keep in mind, though, that dye-based ink technology is steadily improving, and dye-based inks are gaining on pigment-based inks in regard to fade-resistance.

- **Do you do a lot of black-and-white photo printing?** If so, consider a printer that can use photo gray or light black ink.

- **Do the different colored inks for the printer come in separate cartridges?** If the inks come in separate cartridges, then running out of one color of ink requires replacing only that color's cartridge. Over the life of your printer, the savings gained from not having to replace all of the ink whenever a particular color runs out can be quite substantial.

- **Other things to consider** are the physical size of the printer, the speed at which it prints, the noise level, and the cost of the type of ink and paper that the printer uses.

Paper and Ink

Specific papers are designed for specific inks, so you'll usually get the best results if you choose papers that are recommended for use with your printer's ink. Check your printer manufacturer's documentation or Web site for paper recommendations.

Graphics Tablets

IKE A MOUSE, a graphics tablet and stylus provide a way to interact with your computer. A tablet has ergonomic benefits over a mouse: because it's like a note pad and pen, as shown in Figure 5.19, the tablet/stylus combo places less stress on your wrist. Many people also find a stylus easier to control than a mouse. A further advantage is that the tablet, unlike a mouse, can be sensitive to pen pressure, and this can open up a world of possibilities for your photo editing and graphics creation work.

Tablets come in a variety of sizes and levels of sophistication. Wacom, the leading manufacturer of graphics tablets, offers several different tablets in a wide range of sizes. For example, Wacom's Graphire model comes in two sizes, 4 inch × 5 inch and 6 inch × 8 inch; and Wacom's Intuos starts with a 4 inch × 6 inch model and goes all the way up to a whopping 12 inch × 19 inch. The Intuos models also have more levels of pressure sensitivity than the Graphire and several programmable controls that the Graphire lacks.

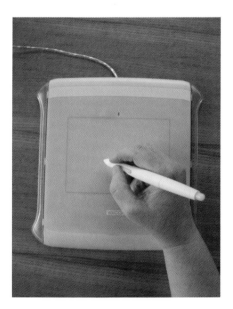

Figure 5.19

A graphics tablet and stylus in use.

Bigger Isn't Always Better

If you're considering a tablet larger than 6 inch × 8 inch, you may want to hold back. Besides being hard to store, a large tablet can be unwieldy and uncomfortable to use. For scrapping purposes, you really don't need a large tablet.

Head over to www.wacom.com and check out what's available. At the time this book is being written, a small Graphire tablet costs only US$99 (or even less if you shop around), and comes bundled with a not-quite-current version of Photoshop Elements, Corel Painter Essentials, and a few other goodies.

Fumerols, Geothermal, Pools, , Paint Pots, Canyon,
Wild Life, Rapids, Old Faithful,, ... and more
June 2007

YELLOWSTONE
NATIONAL PARK

"Yellowstone National Park" layout by Terry Maruca.

6

Photo Editing Fundamentals

ICTURE YOURSELF IN YOUR own digital darkroom, editing your photos so that they look their best. In this chapter, you'll explore the basics of photo editing: straightening a slanted horizon, adjusting color and sharpness, eliminating scratches and blemishes, and cropping for the best composition.

Rotating and Straightening

MANY TIMES YOU'LL FIND that the photos you scan or offload from your digital camera aren't quite straight, or maybe you took a photo in portrait orientation and now your image seems to be lying on its side. All image editors (and most photo album applications) provide tools for rotating and straightening your images.

Rotating

The default orientation of a digital photo is landscape orientation, where the image's width exceeds its height. So what do you do when you take a photo in portrait orientation? Getting portraits and images, like that shown in Figure 6.1, into an upright position is easy—you just need to rotate them 90°.

Figure 6.1

An image that needs to be rotated into portrait orientation.

Some image editors have special commands just for cases like this. Here's what you'd use in Paint Shop Pro Photo X2 and Photoshop Elements 6.0:

Paint Shop Pro Photo X2

Image > Rotate Left

Image > Rotate Right

Photoshop Elements 6.0

Image > Rotate > 90° Left

Image > Rotate > 90° Right

There are other, more general ways to get the orientation right as well, and all image editors include one or more means of freely rotating an image. Here are the commands and tools you'd use for rotating an image in Paint Shop Pro and Photoshop Elements:

Paint Shop Pro Photo X2

Image > Free Rotate

Pick tool

Photoshop Elements 6.0

Image > Rotate > Custom

Image > Transform > Free Transform

Commands for freely rotating an image usually include settings for rotating 90° clockwise (right) or counterclockwise (left), 180°, and maybe 270°. In addition, free rotation commands have a control that lets you enter other values, enabling you to tilt your image any way you like.

Rotation tools also enable you to freely rotate an image. When a rotation tool is active, you can drag with the mouse to rotate your image. (See your application's documentation for precise instructions.) Figure 6.2 shows an image being freely rotated in Photoshop Elements' Free Transform.

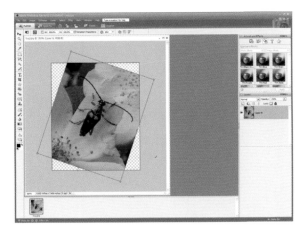

Figure 6.2

Images can be freely rotated using an image editor's rotation tool.

Mirroring and Flipping

Your image editor might also include commands for changing the original photo to its mirror image or for flipping the photo top to bottom. In Paint Shop Pro Photo X2, use Image > Mirror and Image > Flip. In Photoshop Elements 6.0, use Image > Flip Horizontal and Image > Flip Vertical.

Straightening

In more cases than you might like to imagine, a photo's horizon line is tilted. And in the case of scanned images, the scan may be askew because the original photo wasn't placed perfectly straight on the scanner's bed.

It's quite easy to fix photos and scans that aren't level. Your first impulse might be to use your application's free rotate command or rotation tool to get the angle right. That would work, but it usually requires quite a lot of care and guesswork. An easier solution is to use your image editor's dedicated straightening command or tool:

Paint Shop Pro Photo X2

Straighten tool

Photoshop Elements 6.0

Image > Rotate > Straighten Image

Image > Rotate > Straighten and Crop Image

Figure 6.3 shows an example image being straightened with Paint Shop Pro Photo's Straighten tool. With this tool or any similar tool or command, you position the tool's guide line along the horizon or other line that should be perfectly horizontal or perfectly vertical. Figure 6.4 shows the straightened result after cropping.

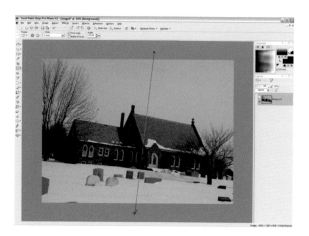

Figure 6.3

Straightening a photo with Paint Shop Pro Photo's Straighten tool.

Figure 6.4

The straightened result.

Quick Fixes

GETTING YOUR PHOTO STRAIGHT or in the proper orientation is only the first step. Almost all digital photos need some adjustment to their color and contrast. In addition to including commands for photographers who want to have full control over these adjustments, most image editors also include automatic photo correction commands that anyone can use with ease.

If you don't know a lot about digital photography—or sometimes even if you do—you'll find your image editor's automatic photo correction tools quite useful. Some editors provide the means for a really quick fix. For example, Paint Shop Pro Photo users can try zapping their photos with the One Step Photo Fix command or, for a little more control, Smart Photo Fix. Although a quick fix will sometimes give unacceptable results, in many cases your photo is markedly improved. For example, notice the improvement in color and contrast shown in Figure 6.5, where Smart Photo Fix is being applied to a photo straight from the camera. The original version appears on the left with the fixed version on the right.

For a little more control, try using individual correction commands. In most cases, this sequence of command types yields the best result:

1. Color balance
2. Contrast enhancement
3. Saturation enhancement

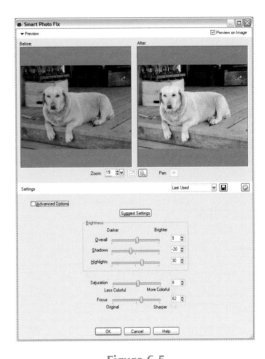

Figure 6.5

Many photos can benefit from your image editor's quick-fix tools.

Color balance corrects the color of your photo. *Contrast enhancement* corrects contrast (the difference between dark tones and light tones), providing your photo with more definition. After correcting the contrast, you'll usually find that the colors are washed out. *Saturation enhancement* can put some verve back into those colors.

The reason you'd want to use the separate commands, rather than your image editor's automatic correction command, is so you can tweak the settings to best suit the specific photo. For example, you might want to increase or decrease the strength of the contrast adjustment. Or, if your photo is a portrait, you'll want to make sure the saturation enhancement doesn't increase the saturation to unnatural levels.

Here's a list of quick-fix photo improvement commands available in Paint Shop Pro Photo and Photoshop Elements, including one-step fixes and commands that allow tweaking:

Paint Shop Pro Photo X2

Adjust > One Step Photo Fix

Adjust > Smart Photo Fix

Adjust > Color Balance

Photoshop Elements 6.0

Enhance > Auto Smart Fix

Enhance > Auto Levels

Enhance > Auto Contrast

Enhance > Auto Color Correction

Paint Shop Pro Photo X2 and Photoshop Elements 6.0 also have special modes dedicated to quickly fixing photos. In Paint Shop Pro Photo X2, go to View > Express Lab, and in Photoshop Elements, go to the Quick Fix tab of the workspace. Figure 6.6 shows Express Lab, and Figure 6.7 shows Quick Fix.

Figure 6.6

Paint Shop Pro Photo X2's Express Lab.

Figure 6.7

Photoshop Elements' Quick Fix tab.

Noise Reduction

DIGITAL PHOTOS CAN INCLUDE quite a bit of *noise*—random dots of color scattered throughout the image. This is particularly common in photos that are somewhat underexposed or contain large areas of blue. Figure 6.8 shows a portion of a photo that exhibits a good deal of noise.

Figure 6.8

Digital photos can be marred by noise.

Image editors provide one or more commands for reducing noise and other specks, such as dust spots on scanned images. Here are a few of the possibilities in Paint Shop Pro Photo X2 and Photoshop Elements 6.0:

Paint Shop Pro Photo X2

Adjust > Digital Camera Noise Removal

Adjust > One Step Noise Removal

Adjust > Add/Remove Noise > Despeckle

Adjust > Add/Remove Noise > Edge Preserving Smooth

Adjust > Add/Remove Noise > Median

Adjust > Add/Remove Noise > Salt and Pepper Filter

Photoshop Elements 6.0

Filter > Noise > Despeckle

Filter > Noise > Median

Filter > Noise > Reduce Noise

Each of these methods works by blurring small areas that contrast with surrounding areas so that those areas of high contrast blend into the surrounding areas. Some noise reduction commands, like Paint Shop Pro's Edge Preserving Smooth, try to maintain edges while blurring more random areas of contrast. Some, like Median, affect the whole image, edges and all. Whenever you use a noise reduction command that has adjustable settings, try to use the smallest setting you can so that you don't also lose real image details along with the noise.

Blurring and Sharpening

THE AMOUNT OF SHARPNESS in a photograph can create differences in mood. Subjects in sharp focus grab your attention, and subjects in soft focus seem dreamy or romantic. The amount of focus for the parts of the photo other than the subject also affects the feel of your photo. For example, compare the photos in the layout in Figure 6.9. In the top photo, the blurred background and blurring of the animals' legs produce a sense of motion and speed, with the details of the background unimportant. In the bottom photo, the subject and all other areas of the photo are in sharp focus, providing a sense of rest and place.

Figure 6.9

"Team Roping" layout by Angela M. Cable, demonstrating how focus can affect the mood of a photo.

You can control sharpness with your camera. For example, to get motion blur you can set your shutter speed to a relatively long interval. You can also modify the sharpness of your photo (or parts of your photo) using the blurring and sharpening tools and commands available in your image editor.

Gaussian Blur

Most image editors have several blurring commands. The one blurring command that's most useful for photos is Gaussian Blur.

In Chapter 5, you saw how you can use a wide lens aperture to produce a photo with a shallow depth of field, keeping the subject in focus and blurring objects that are not near the subject. With Gaussian Blur, you can simulate a shallow depth of field by selecting the foreground and background in your photo and blurring them, leaving the subject sharp. Compare the photo in Figure 6.10, where the subject, the foreground, and the background are all sharp, with the version in Figure 6.11, where the foreground and background are blurred with Gaussian Blur.

You control the amount of blurring with Gaussian Blur's single control, labeled Radius or Amount, depending on which image editor you're using. Figure 6.12 shows the Gaussian Blur dialog box in Paint Shop Pro Photo X2.

Figure 6.10

Photo with the foreground, background, and subject all in focus.

Figure 6.11

Simulated shallow depth of field using Gaussian Blur.

Figure 6.12

Gaussian Blur's single control determines the amount of blurring.

Simulating Depth of Field

In photos with a shallow depth of field, areas in front of the subject as well as areas behind the subject are blurred. Areas that are closer to the subject—whether in front of the subject or behind—are less blurred than areas farther from the subject. Therefore, to get the most realistic simulation of a shallow depth of field, apply different amounts of blurring to different areas of your photo, with most blurring in the areas farthest from the subject.

Here's where you'll find Gaussian Blur in Paint Shop Pro Photo X2 and Photoshop Elements 6.0:

Paint Shop Pro Photo X2

Adjust > Blur > Gaussian Blur

Photoshop Elements 6.0

Filter > Blur > Gaussian Blur

Soft Focus

Your image editor might also include a command for Soft Focus, which produces a dreamy scattered light effect in addition to blurring.

Depth of Field Adjustment

Paint Shop Pro Photo includes an adjustment for simulating depth of field: Adjust > Depth of Field. The controls for this are quite limited, however, and the results are so-so. You'll have much more control—and probably much better luck—using Gaussian Blur to simulate depth of field. (See the brief step-by-step in the Tutorials section of the DVD.)

Unsharp Mask

Image editors usually include several sharpening commands, but the best choices for photo work are Unsharp Mask and High Pass Sharpen. You can use either of these sharpening commands to give a little more definition to digital photos (which tend to be less sharp than film photos) and to restore sharpness to photos to which you've applied noise reduction. Figure 6.13 shows the Unsharp Mask dialog box in Photoshop Elements 6.0.

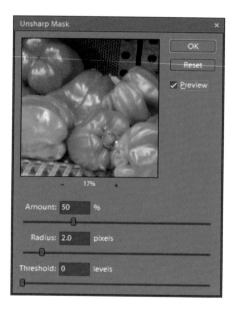

Figure 6.13

Sharpening a photo with Unsharp Mask.

Unsharp Mask has three controls:

- **Amount.** This setting affects contrast. For grainy images, use a low setting (15–20). For other photos, you can have a setting as high as 200. Increase the setting until the sharpening is a bit too strong, and then turn it back down gradually until the sharpening looks rather good. If you see obvious haloes along areas of contrast, the setting is too high. (This control is called Strength in Paint Shop Pro.)

- **Radius.** With high values for Amount, use a low Radius (0.5–1.5). With low Amount values, you'll need higher Radius settings (5 or more). Typically, you'll get good results with Amount set to 100–150 and Radius set to 0.5–1.5.

- **Threshold**. Threshold determines how different two areas need to be before sharpening takes place. When Threshold is set to 0, everything is sharpened. The higher the value for Threshold, the more different two areas must be before sharpening kicks in. For portraits and other photos where areas of smoothness are important, you'll need a relatively high setting for Threshold. In general, it's best to start at 0 and gradually increase the Threshold until you get the result you want. (This control is called Clipping in Paint Shop Pro.)

Here's where to find Unsharp Mask in Paint Shop Pro Photo X2 and Photoshop Elements:

Paint Shop Pro Photo X2

Adjust > Sharpness > Unsharp Mask

Photoshop Elements 6.0

Enhance > Unsharp Mask

Video Display vs. Print

Images that you intend to display on a video monitor should be sharpened so that they appear appropriately sharp when you view them in your image editor. Images that you intend to print may not look sharp enough on paper, though. If that's the case, you should sharpen the image so that it looks slightly oversharpened on your monitor.

Unsharp?

Unsharp Mask's name might seem rather confusing, because you want to sharpen your image, not make it unsharp. This seemingly odd name comes from the process's origins in the physical darkroom, where a blurred version of a negative was used to create sharpening.

Photo Enhancement

SOME DIGITAL PHOTOS NEED more than color correction, noise reduction, or sharpening. These might be scans of old photos that have been physically damaged, photos that include extraneous elements that you'd like to remove, or portraits that feature those creepy glowing irises known as *red eye*. Now we'll take a look at how to correct these types of problems.

Repairing Scratches

Old photos are sometimes marred by scratches, and scans of even pristine photos might sometimes suffer from an inadvertent hair lying on the scanner bed. Scratch removal tools can come to the rescue in these cases and can also be used to remove facial blemishes in portraits.

Here are some tools and commands that are handy for repairing scratches:

Paint Shop Pro Photo X2

Adjust > Add/Remove Noise > Automatic Small Scratch Removal

Scratch Remover tool

Photoshop Elements 6.0

Filter > Noise > Dust & Scratches

Basically, the scratch removing commands work by analyzing your photo and then blurring the parts that the command interprets as a scratch. Scratch removal tools work similarly, except that you control where the scratch removal is applied by dragging the tool along the scratch. A scratch removal tool can be used to eliminate anything long and thin, such as a hair that was inadvertently lying across a print photo on a scanner bed or even actual photo data that you'd like to get rid of. Figure 6.14 shows Paint Shop Pro Photo's Scratch Remover being used to remove telephone lines from a photo.

Figure 6.14

Removing telephone lines with Paint Shop Pro Photo's Scratch Remover.

> **Short Strokes Are Best**
>
> **When using a scratch remover tool, make a series of short drags rather than one long continuous drag. That way you'll have much more control and the result will look more natural.**

Cloning

Cloning is taking image data from one section of an image and copying that data onto another area of the image. All image editors have some kind of cloning tool. Here are the cloning tools in Paint Shop Pro Photo X2 and Photoshop Elements 6.0:

Paint Shop Pro Photo X2

Clone brush

Photoshop Elements 6.0

Clone Stamp tool

One of the handiest uses for cloning tools is to correct blemishes in a photo. Set the source point for the copying by right-clicking, Shift-clicking, or clicking (depending on which application you're using), and then paint to cover the blemish by clicking or dragging while holding down the left mouse button. For best results, use short strokes or dabs rather than long strokes. Figure 6.15 shows a photo in need of cloning, and Figure 6.16 shows some cloning in progress in Photoshop Elements 6.0.

For best results, use a soft edge for your clone brush and adjust the size as needed. Don't hesitate to change the source point or brush size as you go.

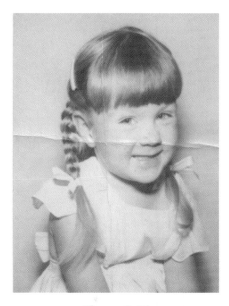

Figure 6.15

A damaged photo in need of cloning.

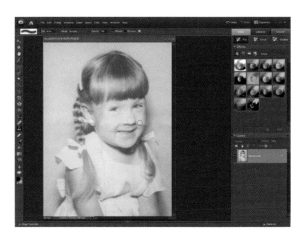

Figure 6.16

Creases and splotches can be eliminated with cloning.

You might also get better results if you reduce the opacity of your brush so that the cloned image data is semi-transparent. That way, you can dab multiple times to build up the effect until you get just what you want. This is an especially good idea when you're working on areas of a person's face, where a delicate touch is key.

Most image editors also include one or more dedicated tools for eliminating objects and for blemish repair. Paint Shop Pro Photo has its Object Remover for removing large objects and the Blemish Remover mode of the Makeover tool for removing smaller objects. Similarly, Photoshop Elements has its Healing brush for removing largish imperfections and Spot Healing brush for smaller imperfections.

Some Uses for Cloning

Besides using clone tools to repair damage to photos, such as cracks, tears, and creases, you can also use clone tools to reduce wrinkles or cover up imperfections on a person's face. You can even remove large areas of a photo, such as electrical wires or your cousin's former spouse.

Dodging and Burning

Dodge and Burn tools can be used to lighten overly dark areas (Dodge) or darken overly light areas (Burn). Typically, these tools are like paintbrushes, but instead of applying paint, these brushes modify the pixels that are already present in your digital image.

To use these tools, set the brush size as you would any other brush tool in your image editor. Set the edge of the brush so that it's rather soft and set the strength of the effect quite low. In some image editors, the setting to use for reducing the strength is labeled Opacity, and settings of 10 (or even less) will probably yield the best results.

Paint over the areas that you want to change. Short strokes or dabs are usually best. If you make a mistake, use your image editor's Undo feature to undo the last stroke, and then reapply.

Retouching Tools

Your image editor may have other photo retouching tools in addition to tools for dodging and burning. These might include brushes for localized blurring or sharpening, brushes for localized adjustments to color and saturation, and brushes for smudging areas of the image together.

Red-Eye Removal

You've probably seen it a lot: those shiny demonic-looking red or greenish pupils that mar portraits of your family, friends, and pets. Don't despair—red eye is something that's easy to fix.

Image editors take two approaches to fixing red eye. One is to use a brush tool. In this case, you set the brush properties and then click on the red-eye area. The other approach is to have a command that pops up a dialog box where you can select the areas to change, and then adjust settings to get just the right effect. Figure 6.17 shows the dialog for Paint Shop Pro Photo's Red Eye Removal command.

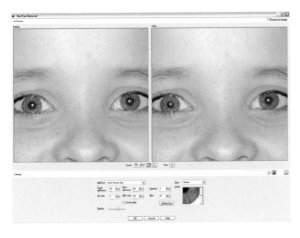

Figure 6.17

Eliminating red eye.

Many image editors include an automatic red-eye removal command. In this case, the command detects areas of red eye and corrects them without any input from the user. This method is sometimes not as successful as those that require the user to do some of the work, but you might want to give it a try and see what you think.

Here's where to find the red-eye removal tools or commands in Paint Shop Pro Photo X2 and Photoshop Elements 6.0:

Paint Shop Pro Photo X2

Adjust > Red Eye Removal

Red Eye tool

Photoshop Elements 6.0

Enhance > Auto Red Eye Fix

Red Eye Removal tool

Although it's not difficult to get rid of red eye, it's even handier to avoid it altogether. Red eye typically occurs when the light of your camera's flash reflects off the retinas of your subject. One way to avoid red eye is simply not to use your flash, but of course, that's not always feasible. Here are a couple of other workarounds:

- ⊙ **If your camera has a pre-flash or red-eye reduction feature, give it a try. The short burst of light before the actual flash causes your subject's pupils to constrict, reducing the amount of light reaching the subject's retinas. However, keep in mind that some of your subjects might find the pre-flash annoying.**

- ⊙ **Use a flash attachment that can be held at a different angle than the head-on angle of the camera lens. This way, the light from the flash won't be directed right into your subject's eyes and reflected back to the camera.**

Cropping and Resizing

OR A FINISHING TOUCH, you may want to change the size of your photo. As you saw in Chapter 3, there are two ways to change an image's size: cropping and resizing. Cropping cuts away some of the original photo. The photograph loses some of its data, but the quality of the image doesn't change. Resizing keeps all of the areas that appeared in the original photo, but quality can be noticeably degraded.

Cropping

Cropping is used primarily to improve the composition of a photo. For example, take the photo shown in Figure 6.18. The little boy is obviously the intended subject here, but he's lost in the surrounding space.

Figure 6.18

A photo in need of cropping.

Now take a look at the cropped version in Figure 6.19. Here the observer's attention is clearly directed to the boy—a much more interesting composition.

Figure 6.19

Cropping directs attention to the subject, creating a more interesting image.

Here are the means of cropping in Paint Shop Pro Photo X2 and Photoshop Elements 6.0:

Paint Shop Pro Photo X2

Crop Tool

Image > Crop to Selection

Photoshop Elements 6.0

Crop tool

Image > Crop

Resizing

When you resize an image, you don't cut any of the image away. Instead, you stretch the image out to make it larger or squash it down to make it smaller. When you increase an image's size, the image editor does an *interpolation*, making its best guess at what the added pixels should look like and then sticking those new pixels in amid the existing pixels. When you decrease an image's size, the image editor chooses pixels to throw away or combine.

Keep in mind that you'll get the best results if you maintain the original image's *aspect ratio* (its ratio of height to width). Also, you'll almost always get better results when decreasing the image's size than when increasing the size.

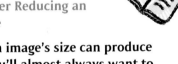

Sharpen after Reducing an Image's Size

Reducing an image's size can produce blurring. You'll almost always want to sharpen your image a bit after reducing its size.

Figure 6.20 shows the Resize dialog box in Photoshop Elements 6.0. And here's where to find the resizing commands in Paint Shop Pro Photo and Photoshop Elements:

Paint Shop Pro Photo X2

Image > Resize

Photoshop Elements 6.0

Image > Resize > Image Size

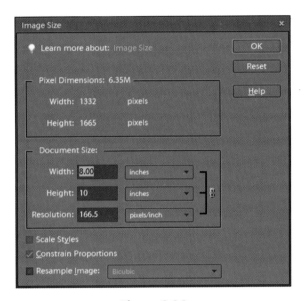

Figure 6.20

Resizing an image.

Most image editors let you change the image size in terms of pixels, percentages, or print size (usually in inches or centimeters and possibly other units). In nearly all cases, the Resize dialog box also gives you the option of changing the image resolution (the number of pixels per inch) either in conjunction with resizing or without any change in your image's dimensions.

Resizing Tools

You might also be able to resize an image or layer with one of your editor's tools, such as Paint Shop Pro Photo's Pick tool or Photoshop Elements' Free Transform. Do any resizing and rotating with such a tool all at once in order to avoid image degradation. In other words, choose the tool and do all your resizing and rotating before selecting another tool.

Changing Resolution without Resampling

To change the image resolution without changing the image's dimensions, be sure to deselect whatever control in your image editor that triggers resampling. In this case, the number of pixels in the image stays the same. The only thing that changes is the instruction that determines how close together the pixels will be packed when the image is printed.

You'll have the option of constraining your image's proportions (aspect ratio). In order to prevent distortion, you'll want to be sure that this option is selected. You'll also have a variety of resizing methods from which to choose. These may include methods like *Bicubic* and *Bilinear*. Bicubic is usually the best option to choose when you want to increase the size of your image. Bicubic might also work well when decreasing the image's size, but if the results are too blurry, try Bilinear instead. Paint Shop Pro Photo also includes a resampling method option called Smart Resize, which analyzes your image and chooses the best resampling method for that image.

A Few Last Words

BEFORE LEAVING THIS CHAPTER, here's one more important tip. Whenever you edit a digital photo or scan, edit a copy rather than the original. Keep the original as is and store it away for safe keeping. That way, you can always go back if you want to make a new attempt at editing the photo. It's possible to make a mistake from which it's hard to recover, or at some time in the future you may learn a new editing technique that can produce better results than current techniques. In cases like this, you'll be happy to have a copy of the original photo on hand.

One last "last word" on basic photo editing: Never work on a JPEG version of your image. JPEG uses a form of compression that throws away bits of your image. The image quality is diminished each time you edit a JPEG image, save it to disk, and close the image. To avoid this, save your edited photo in a format that uses no compression or that uses a type of compression that doesn't throw away image data. Appropriate formats include TIFF, PNG, and the native format of your image editor, such as Paint Shop Pro Photo's PspImage format or Photoshop Elements' PSD format.

My dream for you is to neve r feel pain you can't bear, and to feel love you cant be without.

My DREAM for you...

"My Dream for You" layout by Doris Castle.

7

Advanced Photo Techniques

PICTURE YOURSELF BECOMING even more adept in your digital darkroom. Now that you've mastered the basics of digital photo editing, it's time to really take control.

In this chapter, we'll look at several advanced photo enhancement methods. We'll begin with a method for better cropping, then go on to a few manual methods for correction of brightness, contrast, and color. Then we'll wrap up with some methods for converting color photos to black and white.

Better Cropping: The Rule of Thirds

IN CHAPTER 6, "PHOTO EDITING Fundamentals," you saw how cropping can be used to make more interesting compositions. When you look at a photo with an eye to improving its composition with cropping, try using a technique that goes back to ancient times: the Rule of Thirds.

To use the Rule of Thirds as a guide, you divide your photo into thirds both horizontally and vertically. What you want in your composition is to have a strong element of your image at one of the points at which these dividing lines intersect.

For image editors that don't include Rule of Thirds guides, you can easily make your own. Open a new image with a transparent background. Be sure the dimensions of the image are evenly divisible by three (300 × 300 pixels, for example). Select the entire image, then contract the selection by 1 and invert the selection. Paint the selection with a bright color. Turn off the selection and then draw straight lines to divide the image into thirds both horizontally and vertically. The result should look something like what you see in Figure 7.1 (where the checkerboard pattern isn't part of the image but simply an indication of transparency).

Figure 7.1

Rule of Thirds guide: made with lines dividing the image into thirds, horizontally and vertically.

Save the image in a file format that supports transparency, such as your image editor's native file format or PSD.

When you want to use your Rule of Thirds guide, open the guide and the photo that you want to crop. Copy the Rule of Thirds guide and paste it into the photo as a new layer. (You can then close the Rule of Thirds guide file.) The result will look something like what you see in Figure 7.2.

Figure 7.2

The Rule of Thirds guide pasted in as a new layer.

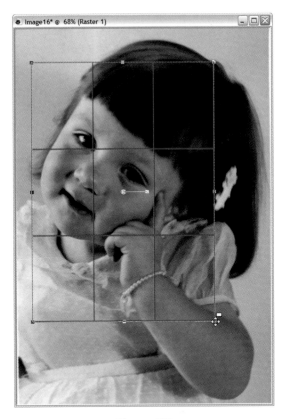

Figure 7.3

Finding the right composition.

Use your image editor's Pick or Free Transform tool to resize and reposition the pasted-in guide. Try to find a composition that you like where a strong element of the photo is at one of the intersection points of the guide lines, as in Figure 7.3.

When you have a composition you like, use your Crop tool to crop around the outer boundary of the guide (Figure 7.4). Then delete the layer that contains the guide, and you'll have your cropped composition, as in Figure 7.5.

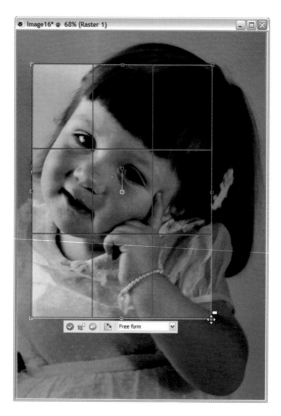

Figure 7.4

Crop around the guide boundary.

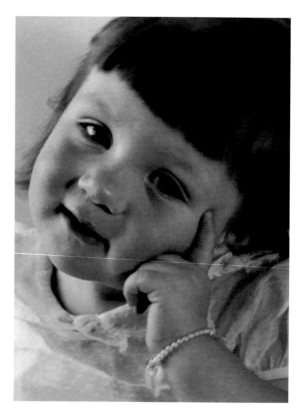

Figure 7.5

The cropped photo.

Emphasizing Points of Interest

When using the Rule of Thirds to help in creating interesting compositions, you don't need to have a point of interest at one of the points of intersection. Instead, you can use the guide lines themselves to line up important horizontal or vertical elements. For example, in a landscape, set the horizon line along one of the Rule of Thirds horizontal guide lines.

Improving Brightness and Contrast

Y OUR IMAGE EDITOR'S AUTOMATIC brightness and contrast adjustment commands might be all you'll ever need for improving your photos. However, as you become more familiar with your image editor—and more particular about your photos—you'll undoubtedly want to look into the more specialized tools for controlling contrast and brightness.

There are two types of brightness and contrast enhancing tools you may want to explore: Levels and Curves.

Levels

The first advanced brightness and contrast enhancer to try out is one typically called Levels (or Level). In most image editors, this command shows you a *histogram*, a graphical representation of the areas of dark and light in your image. Figure 7.6 shows Photoshop Element's Levels dialog. The histogram is the graph below the preview windows.

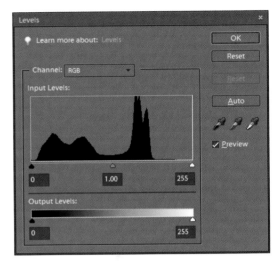

Figure 7.6

The histogram shows your image's areas of light and dark.

The left side of the histogram shows the shadows (the dark areas of the photo), the right side shows the highlights (the light areas), and the middle shows the midtones (the areas with brightness levels in between very dark and very light). The height of the graph at different points shows the amount of image data that occurs in the particular photo at different brightness levels.

Notice that the histogram in Figure 7.6 has no data at either the extreme left side or much of the right side. This indicates that the darkest shadows contain no true black and the highlights contain no true white. The contrast of the image being edited would be improved if its histogram were adjusted so that the darkest pixels are made black (or nearly black) and the lightest pixels are made white (or nearly white). You make these adjustments by moving the triangular slider controls on the left and right below the histogram:

- To darken the shadows, drag the left slider to the area where the left end of the histogram begins.

- To lighten the highlights, drag the right slider to the area where the right end of the histogram begins.

- To adjust the overall brightness of your photo, adjust the middle slider. Moving this control over to the left brightens the image, and moving it to the right darkens the image.

A Little Goes a Long Way

Be conservative in making the left and right slider adjustments. Go too far to the right with the left slider, and you'll lose detail at the shadow end. Too far to the left with the right slider, and you'll lose detail at the highlight end.

In Figure 7.6, the left slider is positioned just to the point where it touches the leftmost end of the histogram, and the right slider is positioned almost to the starting point of the rightmost end of the histogram. The result is darker shadows and whiter highlights.

Here's where you'll find the Levels command in Paint Shop Pro Photo X2 and Photoshop Elements 6.0:

Paint Shop Pro Photo X2

Adjust > Brightness and Contrast > Levels

Photoshop Elements 6.0

Enhance > Adjust Lighting > Levels

Histogram Adjustment

Paint Shop Pro's Levels command doesn't feature a histogram. For a command more like the Levels command in other image editors, Paint Shop Pro users should try Adjust > Brightness and Contrast > Histogram Adjustment instead.

Curves

Another brightness and contrast enhancement command is Curves (called Tone Map or Tone Curve in some image editors). This command is quite powerful and may be either pared down or not be available at all in your image editor. For example, although Photoshop has a full-featured Curves command, Photoshop Elements 6.0 has a somewhat limited version of Curves.

Curves lets you fine-tune brightness and contrast along the whole tonal range, from shadows to highlights, adjusting any number of subranges. To see how, take a look at Figure 7.7, which shows the Curves dialog box in Paint Shop Pro. The most prominent element in the dialog is a graph that represents the modified and the original brightness values of your image.

The graph in Figure 7.7 represents the input and output brightness values along the whole tonal range, with shadows represented at the left side and highlights on the right, with black at the bottom and white at the top. When you open Curves, the graph is a straight line from the lower left to the upper right, because the input and output values match up 1 to 1 before you make any adjustments.

You make adjustments by dragging any node on the curve. When you begin, there are only two nodes, one at the far left (for black) and one at the far right (for white). To add new nodes along the curve, just click on the curve. To lighten pixels at any point, click a node and drag upward. To darken pixels at any point, click a node and drag downward. Figures 7.8 and 7.9 show examples of each.

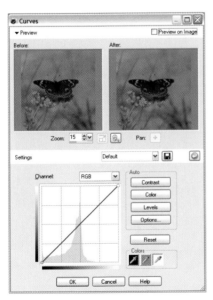

Figure 7.7

Curves features a graph of brightness values.

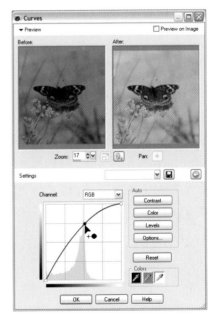

Figure 7.8

Lightening areas of an image with Curves.

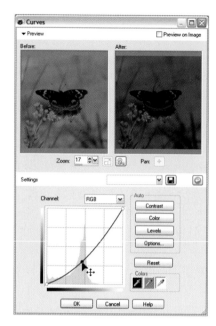

Figure 7.9

Darkening areas of an image with Curves.

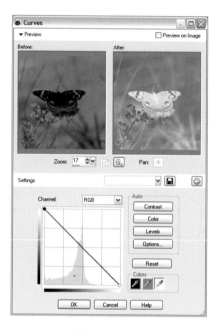

Figure 7.10

Creating a negative version with Curves.

You can even produce a negative version of your photo with Curves. Just drag the leftmost node to the top and the rightmost node to the bottom, completely inverting the original curve. An example is shown in Figure 7.10.

Contrast in any area is affected by the steepness of the graph in that area. The steeper the curve, the higher the contrast. Figures 7.11 and 7.12 show examples of increasing the contrast.

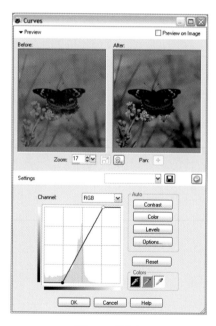

Figure 7.11

Increasing the contrast in an area by increasing the graph's steepness.

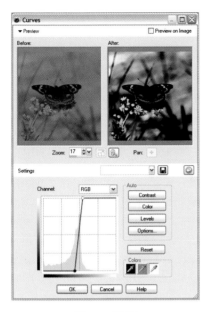

Figure 7.12

Increasing contrast even further.

A commonly used rule of thumb is that a photo benefits by having a slightly S-shaped curve, as in Figure 7.13.

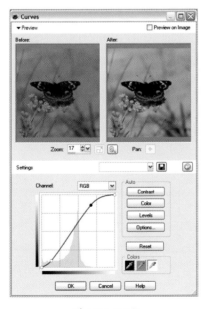

Figure 7.13

An S-curve can benefit many photos.

There are many exceptions to this rule, though, so don't be a slave to it. Especially keep in mind that what this curve does is increase the contrast for the midtones by sacrificing detail in the shadow and highlight ranges. One situation in which an S-shaped curve would be particularly inappropriate is where the photo already has high contrast.

Avoiding Color Shifts

One problem with Curves is that it can produce unintended changes to your image's color. To avoid this problem, try the following technique:

1. **Duplicate the Background layer of your photo.**

2. **On the duplicate layer, apply Curves.**

3. **Set the blending mode of the duplicate layer to Luminance or Lightness.**

4. **Adjust the duplicate layer's opacity until you get the effect you want.**

Here's where you'll find Curves in Paint Shop Pro Photo X2 and Photoshop Elements 6.0:

Paint Shop Pro Photo X2

Adjust > Brightness and Contrast > Curves

Photoshop Elements 6.0

Enhance > Adjust Color > Adjust Color Curves

Manual Color Adjusting

MOST COLOR PHOTOS could do with a little color adjustment. Your photo may have a color cast, perhaps because it was shot with the camera's white balance set inappropriately for the lighting conditions or maybe your camera or scanner is sensitive to some colors more than others. Whatever the case, your image editor provides you with a number of tools for correcting problems with color.

Understanding Color in Digital Images

Full color digital images are represented as combinations of color information. There are several color models, the most common being the Red-Green-Blue (or RGB) model. In this model, all colors are represented as combinations of red, green, and blue. For example, in this method, equal amounts of red and green make yellow, while equal amounts of green and blue make cyan, and equal amounts of blue and red make magenta. If the amount of all three color "channels"—red, green, and blue—are equal, the result is neutral gray.

There are 256 levels of brightness for each of the three color channels, the lowest level being 0 and the highest being 255. If all three color channels have a value of 0, the result is black. If all three have a value of 255, the result is white. Because there are three channels, each with 256 possible values, the total number of colors that can be represented is approximately 16.7 million $(256 \times 256 \times 256)$.

Another way to represent color digitally is with the Hue-Saturation-Lightness (or HSL) model. Like the RGB model, the HSL model also represents colors in three "channels." In this model, there's one channel for hue, one for saturation, and one for lightness.

Hue is pretty much what you might normally think of as color: red, yellow, green, and so on. Saturation is the purity, intensity, or vividness of the color. A totally saturated color is the pure color, a totally unsaturated color is gray, and other saturations give results in between.

Lightness is the level of brightness in your image. Increasing the lightness makes the image brighter, and decreasing it makes it darker.

All or most of the color correcting commands in your image editor make use of one or the other of these two color models. Some affect color balance (the relative amounts of red, green, and blue); others affect hue or saturation.

Common Situations Requiring Color Correction

Probably the most common use for color correcting commands is to eliminate color casts. The color of the objects in your photo is affected by the color of the ambient light at the time your photo was taken. Photos taken indoors under incandescent light will have a yellowish cast. Photos taken outdoors in the shade will have a bluish cast. By adjusting the color balance, you can get rid of the cast. Figure 7.14 shows an example where the yellowish cast is being removed by adding more blue, the opposite of yellow in the RGB color model. (The command used in the example is Paint Shop Pro's Red/Green/Blue.)

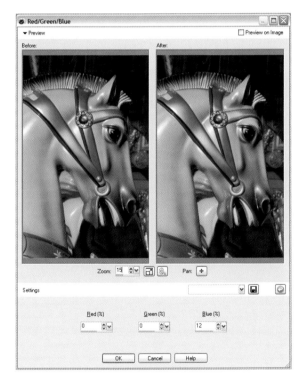

Figure 7.14

One way to eliminate a color cast.

Another common color correction task is saturation adjustment. Photos in which you've increased the brightness can look washed out, for example. In this case, you'd want to increase the saturation to bring back the vividness of the colors. On the other hand, in portraits, the saturation might be too high. In that case, you'd want to bring the saturation down a bit to make the colors look more natural.

Here are a few color and saturation adjustment commands available in Paint Shop Pro Photo X2 and Photoshop Elements 6.0:

Paint Shop Pro Photo X2

Adjust > Color Balance

Adjust > Color > Channel Mixer

Adjust > Color > Red/Green/Blue

Adjust > Hue and Saturation > Hue/Saturation/Lightness

Photoshop Elements 6.0

Enhance > Adjust Color > Adjust Hue/Saturation

Enhance > Adjust Color > Color Variations

Of these, Paint Shop Pro's Channel Mixer is probably the most complex. If you use Paint Shop Pro, you might want to give Color Balance, Red/Green/Blue, or Hue/Saturation/Lightness a try first before tackling Channel Mixer.

Setting Black, White, and Gray Points

As funny as it might sound, you can correct the color in your photos by telling your image editor what parts of the photo should be black, white, or gray. By determining what part of the image should be neutral, some color correction commands can then determine how to adjust the colors overall to get the proper balance, eliminating any color cast.

Commands like these have one or more eyedroppers. You select an eyedropper, then click on a part of the photo that should be neutral. Figure 7.15 shows an example using Photoshop Elements' Remove Color Cast command (Enhance > Adjust Color > Remove Color Cast), which lets you pick an area in your photo that should be pure white, gray, or black.

Here are some of the commands in Paint Shop Pro Photo X2 and Photoshop Elements 6.0 that include eyedroppers for setting black, white, or gray points:

Paint Shop Pro Photo X2

Adjust > Brightness and Contrast > Curves

Adjust > Brightness and Contrast > Levels

Photoshop Elements 6.0

Enhance > Adjust Color > Remove Color Cast

Enhance > Adjust Color > Adjust Color Curves

Enhance > Adjust Lighting > Levels

> **Avoiding Color Casts**
>
> **Even easier than eliminating a color cast is not getting one in the first place. Be sure to consult your camera's manual to see how to adjust white balance for particular lighting situations when you're shooting your photos.**

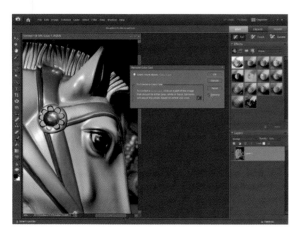

Figure 7.15

Balancing color by selecting a neutral point.

From Color to Black and White

SOME DIGITAL CAMERAS HAVE a black-and-white option, enabling you to capture your photos as black-and-white images rather than in color. Sometimes, though, you'll have a color photo that you'd like to convert to black and white. (And you may even find that the black-and-white versions that your camera produces don't give quite the results you want.) Fortunately, it's very easy to convert a color photo to black and white.

Desaturation

One of the easiest ways to go from color to black and white is to desaturate your image. As you saw earlier in this chapter, saturation is the vividness or purity of a color, ranging from totally pure to totally gray. By setting the saturation as low as it can go, you can change a color photo to black and white.

One problem with this method, though, is that all colors that have the same level of lightness, differing only in saturation and hue, will become the exact same shade of gray. Compare Figures 7.16 and 7.17, where the first is a series of colored blocks and the second is the desaturated version of that same image.

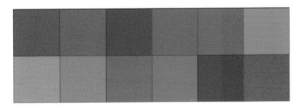

Figure 7.16

Image where all colors are of the same lightness.

Figure 7.17

Desaturated version of the same image.

Of course, you won't find that all of the colors in any of your photographs have the exact same level of lightness, so desaturating your photos will never give you the extreme results shown in Figure 7.17. However, you're almost certain to lose at least some of the detail in your photo if you use desaturation. For some photos, the loss of detail may be barely noticeable, though, so don't rule out desaturation altogether.

Here's a list of desaturation commands in Paint Shop Pro Photo X2 and Photoshop Elements 6.0:

Paint Shop Pro Photo X2

Adjust > Hue and Saturation > Colorize

Adjust > Hue and Saturation > Hue/Saturation/Lightness

Photoshop Elements 6.0

Enhance > Adjust Color > Remove Color

Enhance > Adjust Color > Adjust Hue/Saturation

Converting to Grayscale

Another easy way to convert a color photo to black and white is to change the mode of your image from RGB to Grayscale. A grayscale image has no colors but instead is made up of 256 shades of gray (including pure black and pure white). You'll still lose some detail, since you'll be changing a photo that contains thousands or even millions of different colors into one that contains only 256 levels of gray, but the results are much better than what you get from desaturation, as Figure 7.18 shows.

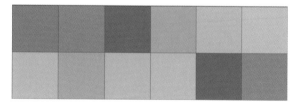

Figure 7.18

Grayscale version of Figure 7.16.

Here are the commands in Paint Shop Pro X2 and Photoshop Elements 6.0 for converting to grayscale:

Paint Shop Pro Photo X2

Image > Grayscale

Photoshop Elements 6.0

Image > Mode > Grayscale

Most of your image editor's special effects and adjustments that are available for color images are also available for grayscale images. An exception, though, is any adjustment that affects color, since a grayscale image has no color. If your image editor produces true grayscale images and you want to introduce color into an image that has been converted to grayscale, you'll first need to change the image mode back to full color. Here's how to do it in Paint Shop Pro Photo X2 and Photoshop Elements 6.0:

Paint Shop Pro Photo X2

Image > Increase Color Depth > RGB - 8 bits/channel

Photoshop Elements 6.0

Image > Mode > RGB Color

Black and White with Channel Mixing

Although channel mixing for color correction can be a bit tricky, when it comes to converting a color photo to black and white, channel mixing is not difficult and can give some incredibly nice results. Paint Shop Pro Photo X2 and Photoshop Elements 6.0 each has a channel mixing command that can be used to create black-and-white effects:

Paint Shop Pro Photo X2

Adjust > Color Balance > Channel Mixer

Photoshop Elements 6.0

Enhance > Convert to Black and White

Recall that in the RGB color model, colors are represented as three channels: one red, one blue, and one green. Each pixel in your photo has values for each of these channels, with 256 possible values for each channel, ranging from 0 to 255. Now, a grayscale image has 256 shades of gray, including black (with a value of 0) and white (with a value of 255). So a channel can be represented as a grayscale image.

That might sound more than a little abstract, so let's look at an example. We'll make use of Paint Shop Pro's ability to split a color image into its separate channels. Figure 7.19 shows a full color image, and Figures 7.20 through 7.22 show the separate color channels for that image.

Figure 7.19

A color image.

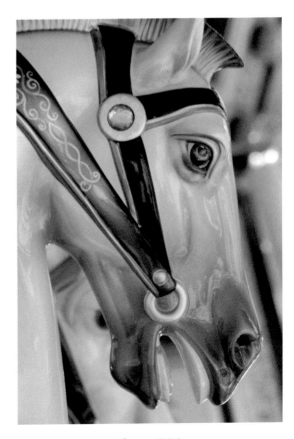

Figure 7.20

The image's Red channel.

Figure 7.21

The image's Green channel.

Figure 7.22

The image's Blue channel.

Each of the channels looks like a grayscale image, but each one is different from the others. Channel mixing enables you to create a black-and-white version of your image that uses any one of the channels or any combination of the channels to create a black-and-white version of your color image.

Converting the photo in Figure 7.19 to grayscale gives you the result in Figure 7.23. Compare that to the version in Figure 7.24, a combination of 76 percent of the Red channel, 42 percent of the Green channel, and −18 percent of the Blue channel.

Figure 7.23

Grayscale version of Figure 7.19.

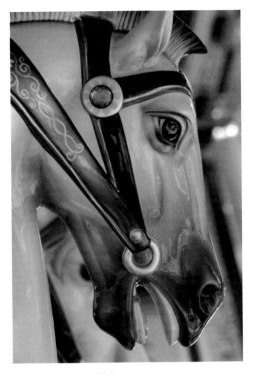

Figure 7.24

Channel Mixer version: 76 percent red, 42 percent green, and −18 percent blue.

To perform channel mixing in Paint Shop Pro Photo X2, start Channel Mixer. Choose the monochrome setting, then adjust the percentages for each of the color channels, being sure that the percentages total 100 percent if you don't want to affect the photo's overall brightness. (Total percentages higher than 100 increase brightness; totals less than 100 decrease brightness.) Figure 7.25 shows the Paint Shop Pro version of Channel Mixer being used on a portrait.

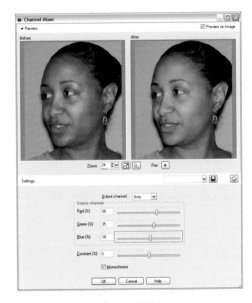

Figure 7.25

Paint Shop Pro Photo X2's Channel Mixer in action.

For Photoshop Elements 6.0, start Convert to Black and White (shown in Figure 7.26). Then drag the Adjustment Intensity sliders to get the effect you want.

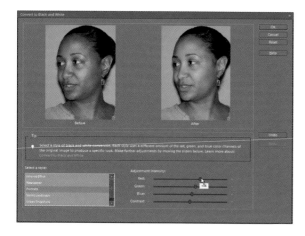

Figure 7.26

Photoshop Elements 6.0's Convert to Black and White command.

Easy Black and White

Paint Shop Pro Photo X2's new Black and White Film effect is an easy way to get good black and white from color. Behind the scenes, this command works a lot like Channel Mixer, but some people find the interface of Black and White Film more intuitive than the interface for Channel Mixer. (Black and White Film is found under Effects > Photo Effects.)

Choosing Channels

In most photos, a lot of detail is contained in the Green channel. For landscapes and other photos where detail is important, maximizing the Green channel is usually ideal. For portraits, though, you don't want to emphasize facial blemishes, pores, and wrinkles, so in these cases be careful using the Green channel.

The Blue channel often contains quite a bit of noise. Most of the time, it's a good idea to minimize use of the Blue channel.

In the portrait in Figure 7.25, for example, very good results come with settings of 55 percent red, 35 percent green, and 10 percent blue.

Tip

Photoshop Elements 6.0 users can easily get appropriate values for Convert to Black and White by choosing one of the standard settings listed on the left of the dialog.

Variations on Black and White

BEFORE LEAVING THIS CHAPTER, let's look at a few variations on black and white that can provide something extra in your layouts. We'll be begin with simple tinting, then look at other kinds of colorizing, and end with a nice effect where a photo frames itself.

Tinted Black and White

Normal black and white is great for many layouts, but sometimes you'll want something just a little different. Maybe you want to simulate the old fashioned look of sepia, or maybe you just want a monochromatic color version of your photo. You can get either of these effects by tinting your photo.

Some tinting commands let you directly tint your color photo without first converting it to black and white. That's usually fine, but in some cases you might get better results by converting to black and white first, since doing so enables you to improve the brightness and contrast of your untinted black-and-white version before doing any tinting.

Figures 7.27 and 7.28 show examples of tinted photos. In Figure 7.27, the photo shown in Figure 7.24 has been given the dull yellowish tint of an old-fashioned sepia print. In Figure 7.28, the same photo is given the pale greenish-blue tint of a cyanotype print.

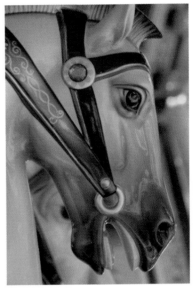

Figure 7.27

The photo in Figure 7.24 with sepia tinting.

Figure 7.28

The photo in Figure 7.24 with cyan tinting.

Any command that adjusts hue and saturation can be used to tint a black-and-white photo. Paint Shop Pro's Black and White Points, when Preserve is unchecked, can also be used to tint a photo. Your image editor might also have one or more commands specifically designed to tint photos.

Figure 7.29 shows an example layout that features a tinted black-and-white photo.

Tinting with Layers

You can also tint a photo by adding a new layer above the photo, filling that layer with the color you want for your tinting, and then setting the blending mode of the upper layer to Color.

Figure 7.29

Layout featuring a tinted photo ("Teddy" by Roberta D'Achille).

Colorizing Black and White

Have you seen photos from say the 1950s where the photographer skillfully (or maybe not so skillfully) colorized a black-and-white photo by hand? You can get the same sort of effect by "painting" on top of your black-and-white digital photos.

Figure 7.30 shows an example. Here, first a new layer is added above the original black-and-white layer. The blending mode of the new layer is set to Color. Painting on the new layer then adds color without affecting the levels of lightness in the layer below. For the most control, each new color is added on its own layer (with the blending mode of each of these layers set to Color). That way, you can make adjustments to the color or opacity of an individual color layer without affecting any of the other layers.

Example layouts that feature hand-tinted black-and-white photos are shown in Figures 7.31 and 7.32.

Figure 7.31

Layout featuring hand-tinting ("Red Barn" by Angela M. Cable).

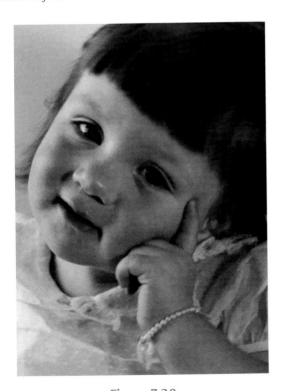

Figure 7.30

A black-and-white photo colored by hand (compare with original in Figure 7.5).

Figure 7.32

Layout featuring hand-tinting ("First Birthday" by Lie Fhung).

Another way to combine color with black and white is to start out with a color photo, duplicate the original layer, desaturate the duplicate layer, and then erase any areas on the duplicate where you'd like the original color to show through. One use for this is as an alternative to cropping (or in addition to cropping) to focus attention on a subject that might otherwise be lost in a busy composition. Figure 7.33 shows an example.

Figure 7.33

Two-layered photo where the top layer is desaturated but the area over the main subject is erased.

Selective color in black-and-white photos can also be used to highlight a feature of the subject, as shown in the layouts in Figures 7.34 and 7.35.

Figure 7.34

Layout featuring selective color ("Fairy Breath" by Lauren Bavin).

Figure 7.35

Layout featuring selective color ("Lindsey and Buster" by Glenda Ketcham).

Floating Color on Black and White

A very nice effect can be created by "floating" a color photo on top of a larger black-and-white version, in effect letting the photo frame itself. An example is shown in Figure 7.36.

To create this effect, start with a color photo. Duplicate the original layer, then return to the original layer and desaturate it. On the duplicated layer, use your application's Free Transform or Pick tool to resize the layer so that the desaturated layer shows through along the edges. When you have the color layer at the size you want and positioned as you like, add a drop shadow to make the smaller color version appear to float above the black-and-white "frame." You may also want to blur the black-and-white layer slightly.

Alternate Frame-Itself Technique

You can also get a nice effect by using this method in reverse: keep the lower layer in color and desaturate the upper layer. You might also try only partially desaturating the upper layer, letting some of the original color tint the upper layer.

Beyond Photo Correction

In the beginning of this chapter, we looked at some advanced photo correction techniques. In the last section, we started looking beyond mere photo correction and began to experiment with artistic photo manipulation. In Chapter 8, "Further Fun with Photos," you'll explore even more ways to do some creative editing with photos, including combining multiple photos into panoramas, montages, and other composites.

Figure 7.36

A photo framed with a black-and-white version of itself.

4 1/2 months, weight: 12 lbs. 14 oz.

about 2 years old

Glenda Irene McKnight

Glenda McKnight

CARD

CORRESPONDENCE   MADE IN CANADA   ADDRESS

I don't have very many photos of me as a baby,
so these photos have always been very special
to me. These photos have lasted many years,
stored in a suitcase under my mother's bed.

"Baby Glenda" layout by Glenda Ketcham.

8

Further Fun with Photos

PICTURE YOURSELF GETTING creative with your photos, modifying your photos to achieve special effects. You combine photos to make montages and panoramas, perform digital face-lifts, and use photos to simulate drawings and paintings.

Compositing Photos

A *composite* IS A COMBINATION of two or more photos, or photos and non-photographic images. The result looks like an original photo. The simplest case of a composite involves placing a figure from a photo onto a new background.

For example, suppose you begin with the portrait in Figure 8.1 and the landscape in Figure 8.2. You could isolate the young woman from the busy background and place it in the landscape to get the result shown in Figure 8.3.

Figure 8.2

A beautiful landscape (photo courtesy of Dmitry Belov).

Figure 8.1

A portrait needing a new background.

Figure 8.3

The figure placed in its new milieu.

Isolating the Figure

How to isolate the figure from the background will depend in part on your specific image editor. All image editors have a collection of selection tools, and those tools are the first to try. If the background is more or less uniform, you'll probably get good results with the Magic Wand, which creates a selection based on the characteristics of the pixel you click, as shown in Figure 8.4.

Figure 8.4

Select uniform areas with the Magic Wand.

Unfortunately, in most cases where you want to isolate a figure from the background, the background is too complex for the Magic Wand to handle. If your image editor has a selection tool that detects edges, use it if the Magic Wand won't do. Here's a list of edge-detecting selection tools in Photoshop Elements and Paint Shop Pro Photo:

Paint Shop Pro Photo X2

Freehand Selection tool in Edge Seeker or SmartEdge mode

Photoshop Elements 6.0

Magnetic Lasso tool

The general method with these tools is to drag the tool around the edge of the figure. Then you can copy the selected figure and paste it onto a new background. Another alternative is to invert the selection, delete the old background, turn off the selection, and paste in your new background as a new layer that you place below the layer containing your isolated figure.

Quick Selection

Photoshop Elements also includes a selection tool that works like a super Magic Wand. With the Quick Selection tool, you can drag over a portion of a complex area that you want included in your selection. You can then refine the selection, adding to it or removing areas that you want excluded from the selection.

Remember to Feather

When isolating a figure from a background, be sure that the edge of your selection has a *feather* that's a few pixels wide. When you copy a selection and paste it into a new image, a feathered edge will gradually fade the edge of the figure from the inside out. This makes the pasted-in figure appear to be part of the target image and not a cutout plopped down on top of the image.

You can set your selection tools so that your selections are created with a feather, or you can add feathering to an existing selection.

Many image editors also include specialized erasing tools for isolating a figure from a background. These include the Background Eraser in Paint Shop Pro and Photoshop Elements, and the Magic Eraser and Magic Extractor in Photoshop Elements. Most of these are tools accessed from Paint Shop Pro's or Photoshop Elements' toolbar. The Magic Extractor is accessed from Photoshop Elements' Image menu.

Photoshop Elements' Magic Eraser is probably the simplest of these tools. It's very much like the Magic Wand selection tool, except that instead of creating a selection based on the characteristics of a pixel that you click on, the Magic Eraser erases a group of pixels based on the characteristics of a pixel you click on. Figure 8.5 shows an example of the Magic Eraser in action.

Figure 8.5

Photoshop Elements' Magic Eraser deletes pixels that resemble the one you click.

The Background Eraser in both Paint Shop Pro and Photoshop Elements is rather sophisticated. With this tool, you set a large brush size and position the center of the brush in an area you want to delete with the edge of the brush overlapping the area you want to keep, as shown in Figure 8.6.

Figure 8.6

The Background Eraser erases the background, leaving only the figure.

The Background Eraser does take a little practice to master, and in your early attempts you may need to Undo every so often, adjust its tolerance setting, and try again. This tool is well worth the effort you put in at first to learn it, though, and we strongly advise Paint Shop Pro users to give it a try.

Photoshop Elements' Magic Extractor is a wonderful tool for isolating figures. Inside the Magic Extractor dialog, you click or drag over portions of the areas that you want to keep and then change modes and click or drag over portions that should be excluded. When you click the Preview button, you'll see the result, as shown in Figure 8.7. You can then use any of the different modes to refine the result.

Yet another approach is to use masks or editable selections to isolate a figure from a background. We won't examine masks and editable selections here because they're rather complex and vary a bit from image editor to image editor. But be sure to consult your image editor's manual or Help file to learn more about these powerful means of isolating figures.

The New Background

Once you have the figure isolated, you're ready to add the new background. You can create a new background with a gradient or pattern, as in Figure 8.8, or you can place the figure on another photo, as you saw in Figure 8.3.

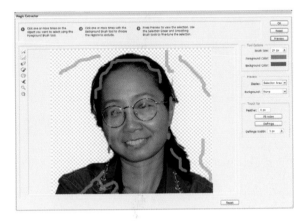

Figure 8.7

Photoshop Elements' Magic Extractor.

Nothing's Perfect

No matter which of these methods you use, be prepared to do a little clean-up erasing and maybe a bit of cloning afterward. None of these methods is fool-proof, and each requires a bit of practice. Once you have some experience with these tools and understand their limitations, you'll find them invaluable.

Figure 8.8

An isolated figure on a gradient background.

To place the isolated figure on a new background, open both the image containing the isolated figure and the image that contains the background. (If you're using a photo for your background, be sure to use a copy and not your original photo.) Then copy the isolated figure and paste it as a new layer in the image that contains the background. Position the pasted-in figure as you want it to appear. The Layers palette for the composited image will then look something like Figure 8.9 in Paint Shop Pro Photo X2 and like Figure 8.10 in Photoshop Elements 6.0.

Figure 8.10

*Layer structure for the composited photo,
in Photoshop Elements 6.0.*

You may then need to do a little tweaking, perhaps blurring the background or adjusting the colors and contrast so that the two layers match more closely. You might also want to use your Dodge and Burn brushes to add some highlights and shadows to the edges of the figure.

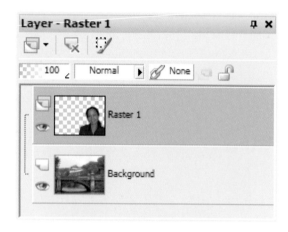

Figure 8.9

Layer structure for the composited photo, in Paint Shop Pro X2.

Photo Montage

A *photo montage* COMBINES photos to create an artistic composition. The photos might be kept distinct, as in Figures 8.11 and 8.12, or they might be blended together, as in Figure 8.13.

Figure 8.12

A montage featuring several versions of the same photo ("Beach" layout by Terry Maruca).

Figure 8.11

A photo montage featuring separate photos ("Nikki and Pebbles" layout by Roberta D'Achille).

Figure 8.13

*A montage featuring blended photos
("Near the Sea" layout by Glenda Ketcham).*

To create a blended montage, begin with a large background image. Next, copy one of your images and paste it as a new layer onto the background image. Position the pasted-in photo, resizing it as needed, and then use your Eraser tool to remove areas you don't want to keep, adjusting the opacity of the Eraser as you go so that the edges gradually fade away. Or use your application's freehand selection tool ("lasso") to select the area you want to keep. Feather the selection, invert it, and delete the area in the inverted selection. Or if you're familiar with masks, you can use one to "erase" areas that you don't want.

Follow the same procedure with the next photo, copying it and pasting it as a new layer above the previously pasted-in photo. Delete the areas you don't want, making sure to gradually fade the edges.

Repeat for any other photos you want to add to the montage. Adjust the opacity and blending modes for each of the layers to get the effect you want. You can also lighten or darken a layer, or adjust the colors or contrast. When you're done, you can merge all the layers together, if you like, and save the finished image. It's also a good idea to keep a copy of the layered version in case you want to make changes to your montage later.

Montages and Montages

Some scrappers refer to a photo montage as a *collage*. Technically, a collage is pretty much what you find in a typical scrapbook layout: photos combined with cut and torn paper and other objects. However, a collection of photos that are combined—particularly one with photos that are subtly blended together—is a *montage*.

Just to make things even more complicated, "montage" is also sometimes used to refer to a photo where the colors of the photo are replaced by tiny photos.

Creating a Panorama

PANORAMAS CAN BE QUITE dramatic. The sweep of a panoramic view can capture the beauty and majesty of a breath-taking landscape. And you don't need a special camera to create lovely panoramas.

Several software applications have a built-in facility for creating a panorama by "stitching" together a series of photos. For example, Photoshop Elements' Photomerge is one means of creating panoramas from a series of individual photos. Figure 8.14 shows an example of a layout featuring a photo-stitched panorama.

If your image editor doesn't include photo stitching, though, you have a couple of options. One is to get dedicated panorama-creation software, such as Autostitch (www.cs.ubc.ca/~mbrown/autostitch/ autostitch.html) or Serif's PanoramaPlus 3 (www.serif.com). Alternatively, you can create panoramas by hand.

To create a panorama by hand, start out by taking two or more photos of a scene. First, take a photo at one end of the scene, pivot to take the next shot, then pivot to take the next shot, and so on. The photos should be shot so that there's quite a bit of overlap between adjacent shots (with a 50% overlap ideal). For this example, let's use the two shots of an urban landscape shown in Figure 8.15.

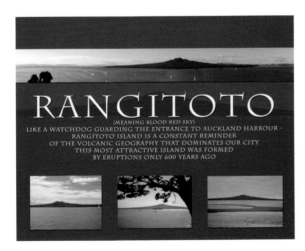

Figure 8.14

A layout featuring a photo-stitched panorama ("Rangitoto" by Lauren Bavin).

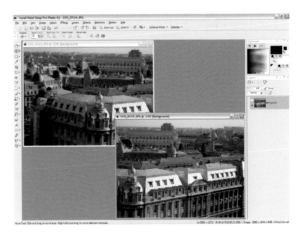

Figure 8.15

Beginning with two separate photos.

Here's how to put the photos together to create a seamless panorama:

1. Open a new image canvas that's large enough to hold both photos side by side. It's a good idea to have some extra vertical space because the photos probably won't line up exactly.

2. Copy the first photo and paste it as a new layer in your new image canvas. Figure 8.16 shows where the first photo is pasted in as a layer over a transparent image canvas. Position the photo as needed.

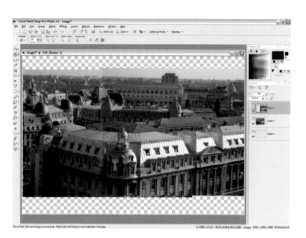

Figure 8.17

Positioning the second photo.

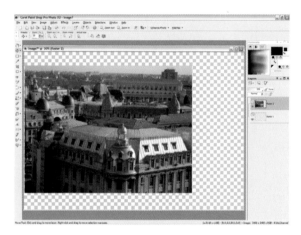

Figure 8.16

Pasting in the first photo.

3. Copy the next photo and paste it as a new layer. Position it as needed. If you need to line the layer up with the previous layer, use a rotation or straightening tool to do so. The result should look like Figure 8.17.

4. If you're combining more than two photos, repeat step 3 as needed.

Lining Up the Photos

To help position the pasted-in layer correctly, temporarily reduce the layer's Opacity so you can see the layer below. When you're finished positioning the layer, reset the layer's Opacity to 100.

Another trick to try is to change the upper layer's blending mode to Difference. When the two layers are lined up correctly, the overlapping areas will appear completely black (or, if the layers' colors don't match exactly, a more or less uniform dark shade with perhaps some highlighted edges showing). When the layers are lined up correctly, change the upper layer's blending mode back to Normal.

5. Use your image editor's Eraser tool with a soft brush setting to make the seams between the image layers less sharp. You can also use your cloning tool to edit the seams and to add content if the image canvas shows through along the edges of the image.

6. If necessary, adjust the color, brightness, and contrast of the layers so that they match one another. Then crop your panorama image so that none of the image canvas is left showing. The final result should look like Figure 8.18.

You can also create a panorama-like effect by cropping a landscape photo so that the result is much wider than it is high. Figure 8.19 shows a layout that features a pseudo-panorama of this type. Landscapes with strong horizontal elements are best for this technique.

Shots for Stitched Panoramas

For a full-size panorama, you'd almost certainly want to use a tripod and your camera's exposure lock feature when taking your series of photos, to be sure that the edges of your photos line up precisely. For panoramas that are not full-size—such as those featured in a scrapbook layout—you can probably get away with much less precision. In this case, handheld shots will probably do fine, but do lock the exposure if your camera has that feature.

Figure 8.18

The completed panorama.

Boar's Tusk and antelope, Sweetwater County

Figure 8.19

A layout featuring a cropped-photo panorama ("Wyoming: Living the Legends" by Angela M. Cable).

Digital Face-Lift

I N THIS SECTION, you'll see how to use your image editor's warping and cloning tools to return a middle-aged woman to her youth. Begin with a photo like the one in Figure 8.20. We'll give a general outline of the method here. You can adapt this general method for use with the tools provided in your specific image editor.

Now for the fountain of youth:

1. Begin by choosing your image editor's warping tool. Choose the mode that lets you push pixels around by dragging, and set the brush size rather large. Then use the large brush to lift the woman's sagging cheeks, as shown in Figure 8.21.

Figure 8.21

Raising the cheeks.

Figure 8.20

The original photo.

2. Again using a large brush, push the droopy jowls up, as shown in Figure 8.22.

Figure 8.22

Eliminating the jowls.

3. Reduce the brush size, and then gently pull up the corners of the mouth just a little, as shown in Figure 8.23.

Figure 8.23

Lifting the corners of the mouth.

4. Now for a step many folks forget about: fixing the neck. Go back to a large brush, and then push the neck in a little, as shown in Figure 8.24.

Figure 8.24

Slimming the neck.

5. Next, remove blemishes and reduce wrinkles using any of the blemish-repairing tools discussed in Chapter 6, "Photo Editing Fundamentals." In Paint Shop Pro Photo X2, these include the Scratch Remover tool and the Blemish Remover mode of the Makeover tool. In Photoshop Elements 6.0, the Healing Brush and Spot Healing Brush are available. And nearly every image editor includes a Clone brush. Whatever tool you use, remember the neck as well as the face.

6. As you're working, change the brush size of your blemish-repairing tools as needed. It's usually best to dab with the brush rather than drag. Keep in mind that the idea here isn't to totally eliminate every line and crease. Even young people have a few lines, and you want to be sure that your edited image looks like a real person, not like a circus clown or a store mannequin. Figure 8.25 shows a side-by-side comparison of the original photo and the completed face-lifted version.

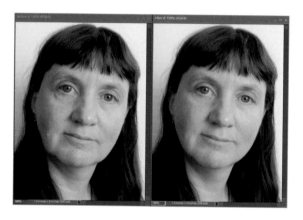

Figure 8.25

Before (left) and after (right).

Grade-A Warp Tools

Of the image editors we're familiar with, probably the ones with the best warping features are Paint Shop Pro Photo, with its Warp Brush, and Photoshop and Photoshop Elements, with their Liquify effect. There are warping tools or filters in many other image editors, but their power and responsiveness don't really match those of the warping features of Paint Shop Pro Photo, Photoshop, and Photoshop Elements.

Drawings and Paintings from Photos

EVERY IMAGE EDITOR INCLUDES filters and special effects for transforming photos into drawings and paintings. Some of these produce some stunning effects, but others leave much to be desired. Some plug-in filters also produce artistic effects, and we'll look at a few in Chapter 10, "Enhancing Your Pages with Filters and Layer Styles." You don't absolutely need dedicated artistic filters to produce drawings and paintings from your photos, however. You can also produce some nice artistic effects by hand.

In this section, we'll go over general outlines for how to achieve some of these effects.

Digital Drawings

Of course, you can create digital drawings purely by hand. With your image editor's painting tools, you can adjust brush settings to get a brush that simulates a pencil, chalk, pastels, or charcoal. It's easy to make a tracing from a photo as well, especially if you have a graphics tablet and stylus. First add a new layer above your photo, fill the new layer with white or gray, and lower the layer's opacity so you can see the photo beneath. Then add another layer for the actual tracing, and trace away. Figure 8.26 shows an example in Paint Shop Pro, with the layer structure indicated in the layer palette at the bottom-right of the figure. Figure 8.27 shows a sample tracing once the semi-transparent layer is changed to full opacity and a paper texture is added.

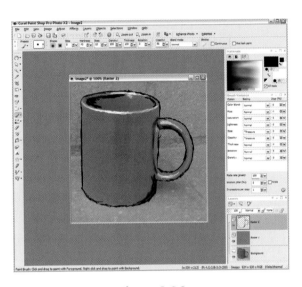

Figure 8.26

Using layers to trace an image.

Figure 8.27

Example of a tracing.

**Adding Your Tracing
to a Layout**

**It's easy to add your tracing to a paper
or a tag in a layout. Simply copy the
upper tracing layer all by itself, and
paste the copied layer into your layout
as a new layer. Then position the
pasted-in tracing, resize it, or rotate
it as needed.**

You can also create digital drawings without touching a brush. There are plenty of variations on this technique, but here's one that generally works rather well:

1. Begin with a color or black-and-white photo that has a simple, light-colored background, like the one in Figure 8.28. If it's a color photo, convert it to grayscale or use channel mixing to make a black-and-white version. You'll usually get the best results if you increase the contrast, as shown in Figure 8.29.

2. Duplicate the photo layer. Make this layer a negative version of your original image and set the layer's blending mode to Dodge (in Paint Shop Pro) or Color Dodge (in Photoshop Elements). The image looks almost completely white, with perhaps some black also showing.

3. Use Gaussian blur set to a value somewhere between 3 and 10. The image will look like Figure 8.30. If you like this look as is, skip to step 6.

Figure 8.28

The original photo.

Figure 8.29

A higher-contrast version.

Figure 8.30

Blurring the negative brings out the edges.

Figure 8.31

Pencil marks added.

4. To add some pencil markings to your sketch, duplicate the bottom layer again. On your new middle layer, add some monochrome noise (about 25% Gaussian noise).

5. Set the layer's blending mode to Darken. Then use a motion blur with the angle of the blur set somewhere between 45 and 55, with the intensity of the blur set to whatever value gives you the effect you want. The exact result you get will depend on what image editor you're using. Figure 8.31 shows the result in Photoshop Elements 6.0.

6. Optional: Merge the layers, and then adjust the brightness and contrast with Levels or Curves.

Figure 8.32 shows a sample layout that features a digital drawing.

Figure 8.32

A layout featuring a digital drawing ("Dare to Dream" by Lori J. Davis).

Digital Paintings

Your image editor probably includes a host of special effects that can be applied to a photo to create painting-like variations. For example, Figure 8.33 shows Paint Shop Pro's Brush Strokes effect being applied to a photo of a rose, using the effect's default settings. Figure 8.34 shows Photoshop Elements' Watercolor effect being applied to the same photo.

Figure 8.34

Photoshop Elements' Watercolor effect.

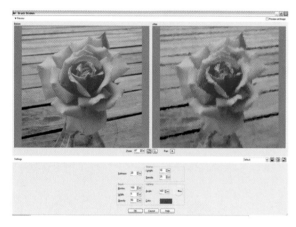

Figure 8.33

Paint Shop Pro's Brush Strokes effect.

You can also create your own painting-like effects by using one or more adjustments or effects that aren't specifically designed to produce artistic effects. Let's look at a simple example using Paint Shop Pro, beginning with the photo in Figure 8.35.

Figure 8.35

A photo ready to be turned into a painting.

1. Open your photo image. (Even improperly exposed or blurry photos can work with this technique.)

2. Duplicate the Background layer. Turn off the visibility of the top layer for now, and make the lower layer the active layer. With the lower layer active, apply a noise-reducing command to blur the detail of your image. Figure 8.36 shows Paint Shop Pro's Salt and Pepper noise-reducing adjustment being applied, but Median—which is also available in Photoshop Elements—would also do the trick. No matter which noise-reduction method you use, be sure to use settings that are much more extreme than what you'd use for normal noise reduction.

3. Make the top layer visible and active. Apply Effects > Edge Effects > Find All. The result will look something like what's shown in Figure 8.37.

Figure 8.37

Find All reveals the edges.

Figure 8.36

Eliminating detail with a noise-reduction adjustment.

4. Now change the blend mode of the upper layer to Multiply and adjust its opacity until you get an effect you like. Figure 8.38 shows the results for our rose photo.

Figure 8.38
The completed painting.

This is just one simple example. Try other blur, noise-reduction, and edge-detecting commands alone or in combination to produce other painting-like effects. Be sure to try different blending modes and opacities when you combine different layers to produce your digital paintings. Experiment and see how easy and fun it can be to turn photos into paintings!

Part III
Adding to Your Toolbox

Photo taken "somewhere" near Wells, NY

My FAVORITE Past time

LEISURELY PHOTO DRIVES
One of my favorite things to do is to just drive around the countryside, with no particular place to go, and to stop along the way taking beauty photos of the scenery.

"My Favorite Pasttime" layout by Doris Castle.

ASTONISHING earth

Grand Canyon Sunset March 12 2007

Creating Your Own Components

PICTURE YOURSELF CREATING your own scrapbook components, including papers, mats, frames, tags, brads, eyelets, and fibers. It's easier than you think, and you don't need anything more than your image editor to get started!

General Considerations

CREATE YOUR ELEMENTS at 200 ppi or whatever image resolution you normally use for your layouts. Typically, you'll want to create your elements at the largest size you're likely to need them. For example, you might want a print size of half an inch for a brad or eyelet or three inches in diameter for a circular tag. Remember that to get the proper pixel dimensions you multiply the print size by the ppi value, so a half inch at 200 ppi is 100 pixels, and three inches at 200 ppi is 600 pixels.

Components that include transparency should be saved in your image editor's native file format or in another format that supports transparency, such as PNG. Background papers should be saved as JPEG, TIF, or PNG. If you're creating your components solely for your own use, then use whichever of these file types you prefer. If you intend to share your components with other scrappers, use formats that any image editor can read and that are commonly used in the scrapping community: JPEG for background papers and PNG for anything that includes transparency. Most image editors can also read and write in PSD format, the native format of Photoshop and Photoshop Elements.

Step by Step

Throughout this chapter, we'll take an overall view of how to create your own components. For step-by-step instructions on how to employ some of these techniques in Paint Shop Pro and Photoshop Elements, see the tutorials included on the book's DVD.

Using Clip Art

CLIP ART IS READY-MADE ART that you can incorporate into your own designs. Some clip art comes in the form of vector-based line drawings like the Microsoft Office clip art shown in Figure 9.1. Some are scans of physical line drawings, such as the Dover Art example shown in Figure 9.2, while others are figures isolated from photos, such as the Hemera Photo Objects example shown in Figure 9.3 (where the checkerboard pattern isn't part of the image, but simply indicates transparency).

Figure 9.2

Scanned clip art from Dover Art.

Figure 9.1

Vector-based clip art from Microsoft Office.

Figure 9.3

Photo object from Hemera.

If your image editor supports vector editing, vector-based clip art can be resized, recolored, and otherwise manipulated without any distortion at all. However, even if your image editor doesn't have full support for vectors, you may be able to open vector images and use them in raster format. In that case, you lose the advantages of vectors, but you still can make use of the images.

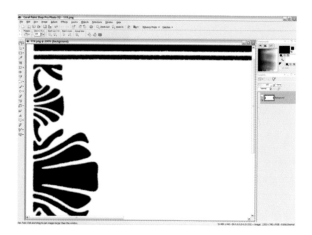

Figure 9.4

Scanned clip art sometimes needs some cleaning up.

Vector Images

Vector-based images are quite different from raster images, such as photos and painted graphics. *Raster images* are made up pixels, the smallest pieces of color that can be represented on your computer screen. *Vector images*, on the other hand, are made up of instructions to your computer for how to draw the image on the screen. Because vector images are instructions and not fixed collections pixels, you can resize or reshape a vector image without affecting the quality of the image.

Scanned clip art is raster-based and is usually made available in one or more of these image formats: BMP, GIF, JPEG, or TIF. Often this sort of clip art could use a little clean up, as the close-up indicates in Figure 9.4.

To get rid of jaggy edges in scanned black-and-white clip art, touch up any straight edges with a hard-edged square brush. For curves, try this method:

1. If necessary, use your image editor's Straightening or Transform/Pick tool to straighten the image.

2. Touch up any obvious gaps or dust spots with your paintbrush.

3. Blur the image slightly with Gaussian Blur.

4. Increase the contrast to get smooth edges using Levels, as shown in Figure 9.5. Moving the left slider to the right maximizes the dark areas, while moving the right slider to the left maximizes white areas.

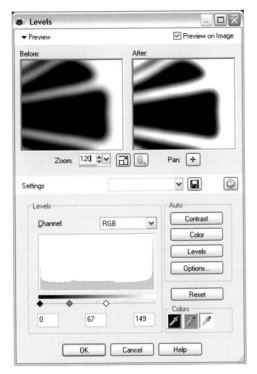

Figure 9.5

Using Levels to create smooth edges.

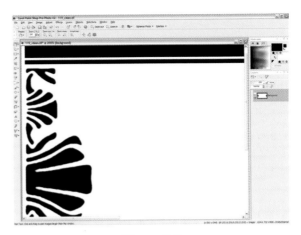

Figure 9.6

Cleaned-up version.

So what can you do with clip art? You can use colored drawings, line art that you color by hand, and photo objects like stickers, pasting them on your page as accents. However, there's more to clip art than stickers. As we'll see later in the chapter, you can also use clip art as the basis for brads, frames, and other components, or to decorate papers and tags.

Notice the difference between what you see in Figure 9.4 and the cleaned-up version shown in Figure 9.6. The image is improved greatly—and with very little effort.

Backgrounds and Papers

THE FOUNDATION OF ANY layout is the background. In this section, we'll look at how to simulate cardstock, patterned paper, and corrugated backgrounds. You'll also see how to create vellum and torn paper.

Simulating Cardstock

Probably the easiest way to create simulated cardstock for a background is to open an image the size of your finished layout. Fill the entire canvas area with the color you want, and then apply a texture to the fill. All sorts of effects can be achieved, depending on what textures you use, either alone or in combination. You can also create textures by adding some noise to your colored paper, and then applying effects and adjustments, such as embossing and blurring. Experiment to see what effects you can create.

Texture

The term *texture* is used in many image editors to refer to simulated surface textures, and that's the meaning here. However, some image editors follow the lead of 3D imaging programs and use texture to refer to what most image editors call a *pattern*. In a case like that, what we refer to here as texture is called a *bump* or *bump map*.

If your image editor supports layer blending modes, you can also add objects that seem to be embedded in your paper. First, create a layer of textured paper. Then add a new layer and place some of the objects that you want to appear embedded in your paper. Add texture to the new layer, then change the blending mode of this layer to Overlay or Soft Light, and adjust the layer opacity until you get the effect you want. If you like, add more layers, each with its own set of objects and blending mode and opacity settings. If the objects on a particular layer appear too distinct, add a blur to that layer. When you're done, you can merge all the layers into a single layer. Figure 9.7 shows an example of a textured paper with embedded objects.

Figure 9.7

Simulated textured paper with embedded objects.

Simple Patterned Paper with Seamless Tiling

Creating a background that's the same size as your finished layout and that has a repeating pattern might be easy, but it isn't efficient. Images with resolutions of 200–300 ppi that are 8.5 × 11 inches or 12 × 12 inches take up an awful lot of disk space. A better approach is to create small seamless tiles.

A *seamless tile* is a small pattern that you can use to fill a large space. It has no noticeable seam, so the tile can be repeated up and down the space without any hint that the whole tile is made up of many copies of a single tile. Suppose you want to make a tile from an image like the one in Figure 9.8. If you were to use this image as a tile, the result would be what you see in Figure 9.9, where the edges of the individual tiles are quite distinct.

Figure 9.9

Original image used as a tile to fill a larger area.

If the tile were seamless, you'd get something like what you see in Figure 9.10, a much more pleasing effect.

Figure 9.8

An image from which to create a tiling pattern.

Figure 9.10

Seamless tile used to fill a larger area.

There are several ways to make a seamless tile. Many image editors include some means of creating a seamless tile from an image. For example, Paint Shop Pro users have Effects > Image Effects > Seamless Tiling. These sorts of seamless tiling effects sometimes give less-than-satisfactory results, though. For some images, you'll get better results if you use a more hands-on method using an offset filter, which was what was used in creating the example shown in Figure 9.10.

Most image editors include an offset filter. Here are some examples:

Paint Shop Pro Photo X2

Effects > Image Effects > Offset

Photoshop Elements 6.0

Filter > Other > Offset

Creating a seamless tile by hand takes a bit of work, so feel free to skim or skip the next part of this section for now. You can always come back later and take a look if you decide you'd like to try creating a seamless tile by hand.

An offset filter itself doesn't create the seamless tile; it just sets things up so you can get rid of the seams by hand. The offset filter is used to split your image into quarters and then swap the quarters so that each of the corners appears in the middle of the image, revealing the seams. A simple offset filter does this splitting and rearranging automatically. For more complex offset filters, you'll need to choose settings so that the horizontal offset is half the width of your image and the vertical offset is half the height of your image. You'll also need to choose a mode that causes the offset image to wrap around. (In Paint Shop Pro, set Edge Mode to Wrap; in Photoshop Elements, set Undefined Areas to Wrap Around.)

Figure 9.11 shows what you'd see in Paint Shop Pro, using the example image from Figure 9.8.

Figure 9.11

Using an offset filter.

After applying the offset filter, the real work begins. Now copy bits of the image and paste those bits over the seams running up and down and across the offset image, or use your clone brush, smudge brush, or paintbrush to blend together the areas around the seams. For instance, Figure 9.12 shows Paint Shop Pro's Clone brush being used to hide the seam in our example image. (Also see the "Tiles Using Offset" tutorial in the Tutorials section of the book's DVD.)

Keep in mind that patience pays off when doing this touch-up work, and that you might want to zoom in on your image. Change the size and opacity of the brush as needed, and when using the Clone brush, reset the sampling area often. Be careful to avoid painting over the edge of the image canvas because doing so will create new seams.

Figure 9.12

Getting rid of the seams with the Clone brush.

When you have the results you want, you might want to apply the offset filter again to set the image back to its original orientation as well as to check that no new seams were introduced.

Plug-In Filters for Seamless Tiles

Several plug-in filters are available for producing abstract seamless tiles or tiles that simulate natural textures. Many of Alien Skin's filters, for example, have a setting that produces seamless tiling effects.

You can also get some nice natural texture tiles by scanning objects, such as cloth and paper, and then using the offset method to make a portion of the scanned image seamless.

File Formats for Tiles

Seamless tiles should be saved as JPEGs if the pattern contains subtle color gradations, such as a photo of grass, sand, or other objects. For tiles that are made up of solid blocks of color with distinct edges, like the stripes and plaids you'll make in the next section, you may get better results saving as a TIF, BMP, or PNG.

Filling an image or selection with a seamless tile varies from image editor to image editor. Here's a summary of how to use your seamless tiles in Paint Shop Pro and Photoshop Elements:

- **Paint Shop Pro Photo X2** lets you use patterns or any open image as a tile. Choose the Flood Fill tool. Click the foreground swatch on the Materials palette, go to the Pattern tab, and select your tile. If the tile image is open or if you saved the tile in your Patterns folder, the tile appears in the pattern selection list. Once you've selected your tile, click in your image canvas with Flood Fill to fill with the pattern.

- **Photoshop Elements 6.0** also has a Fill command. Choose Edit > Fill, select Pattern, and select the pattern you want. Only images that have been defined previously as patterns are available. To define an image as a pattern, open the image and choose Edit > Define Pattern.

Stripes and Plaids

It's easy to make seamless tiles for repeating stripes, and not much harder to make gingham or plaid tiles. For vertical stripes, open an image as wide as you'll need for the repeating pattern of stripes. The image doesn't have to be very tall—in fact, one pixel would be sufficient, although you'll probably want it taller just so you can better see what you're doing. Add colored rectangles to your image for each of the stripes in the pattern. Figure 9.13 shows a simple two-colored example tile, and Figure 9.14 shows the result of using the tile to fill an area.

Figure 9.14

An area filled with the stripe tile.

Figure 9.13

A simple two-colored stripe tile.

For horizontal stripes, make the image tall enough to accommodate the repeating pattern and just wide enough for you to see what you're doing.

For a gingham pattern, begin with a square image canvas large enough for the repeating pattern. Add a colored rectangle to get a stripe pattern, again as in Figure 9.13. Duplicate the layer and rotate only the duplicated layer 90°, as shown in Figure 9.15. Lower the transparency of the duplicated layer to 50%. The result will look something like what you see in Figure 9.16. When used as a pattern to fill an area, this tile yields the results in Figure 9.17.

Figure 9.15

The stripe pattern on a duplicated layer rotated 90°.

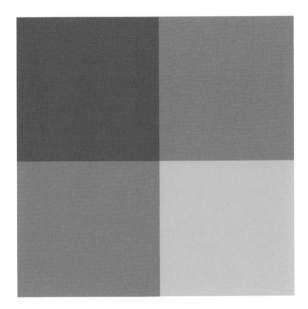

Figure 9.16

*Result of duplicating the layer, rotating it,
and reducing the opacity.*

You create plaids as you do gingham, but you use more stripes. Begin with a square image canvas large enough for the repeating pattern, and then add some stripes, as shown in Figure 9.18. As with gingham, duplicate the layer and rotate only the duplicated layer 90°. Lower the transparency of the duplicated layer to 50%. The result will look something like Figure 9.19. When used as a pattern to fill an area, this tile yields the results in Figure 9.20.

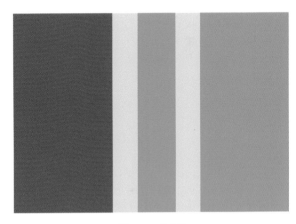

Figure 9.18

Basis of the plaid pattern.

Figure 9.17

An area filled with the gingham pattern.

Figure 9.19

*Result of duplicating the layer, rotating it,
and reducing the opacity.*

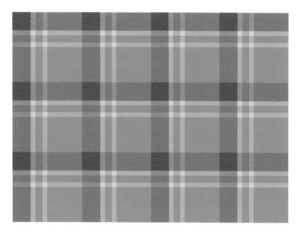

Figure 9.20

An area filled with the plaid pattern.

Save your striped, plaid, and gingham patterns as BMPs, TIFs, or PNGs. This avoids getting murky areas called *artifacts* that could result if these sorts of images are saved as JPEGs. For Photoshop Elements, be sure to save your tiles as patterns. These tiles are seamless, so there's no need to do anything further to them.

Texture and Tiles

You can also add a texture to your stripe, gingham, and plaid backgrounds. For the most flexibility, don't save the texture to your tiles, but instead apply the texture to the filled area. This way, you can use different textures for different layouts without having to save multiple versions of your tiles.

Corrugated Cardboard

To create a corrugated cardboard tile, you simply need to create an image that's filled with a gradient, like the one shown in Figure 9.21.

Figure 9.21

A gradient tile for simulating corrugated cardboard.

Notice how the gradient goes from dark to light, and then from light to dark. When this tile fills an area, it looks like a series of raised and indented bands, as shown in Figure 9.22. This example also has a little monochrome Gaussian noise applied to it to give the cardboard a bit of texture. Applying a filter such as Paint Shop Pro Photo X2's Texture effect or one of Photoshop Elements 6.0's Texture filters is another option for adding a touch of texture to your cardboard.

To create a corrugation tile, you need an image only as wide as one repetition of the corrugation. Fill this image with an appropriate gradient, and then save the image for use as a pattern.

Figure 9.22

An area filled with the corrugated pattern.

Here's how to fill the tile image with a gradient in Paint Shop Pro Photo and Photoshop Elements:

- **Paint Shop Pro Photo X2.** Open an image the size of your tile. On the Materials palette, click the foreground swatch, go to the Gradient tab, and choose the appropriate gradient. Click in the image canvas with Flood Fill.

- **Photoshop Elements 6.0.** Open an image the size of your tile. Choose the Gradient tool. On the tool options bar, choose Reflected Gradient. Click in the center of your image canvas and drag to the right edge. Release the mouse button.

Corrugation Overlay

A gradient of dark and light grays is fine for a corrugation tile. You can fill an area with the tile, and then colorize the corrugated area as needed for your particular layout. Or you can overlay a layer filled with the corrugated tile over a layer containing a paper pattern. Then change the blend mode of the corrugation layer to Overlay to create a corrugated effect on the paper.

Simulating Vellum

Vellum is easy to make. Open a new image with a transparent background. Place a rectangle in your image canvas, using whatever color you want for your vellum. Lower the transparency of the layer so that the rectangle is semi-transparent, as shown in Figure 9.23 (where the checkerboard pattern isn't part of the image, but only indicates transparency).

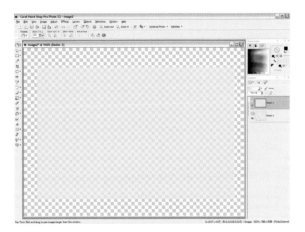

Figure 9.23

Create vellum by lowering the opacity of a colored area.

Shadows Add Realism

When you use the vellum in your layouts, you'll get distinct edges and a nice 3D effect if you add a slight drop shadow to the vellum.

More Realism

For an even more realistic effect, add a black-and-white linear gradient on a layer above your vellum (the same size and position as the vellum). Set the angle of the gradient to about 45°. Then change the blend mode of the gradient layer to Soft Light. This adds a subtle shimmering or shadowy effect. Another possibility is to add a gray cloud-like pattern on a layer above the vellum (again using the same size and position as the vellum), and then change the blending mode of that layer to Overlay and adjust the layer's opacity until you get an effect you like.

Torn Paper

It's easy to get a torn paper effect. Open the image that contains your paper, and then with your image editor's Freehand Selection/Lasso tool, make a rough, jagged selection along the edge where you want the tear, as shown in Figure 9.24.

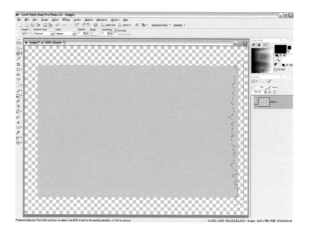

Figure 9.24

Begin with a jagged freehand selection.

Delete the selection and turn the selection off. Then make a new jagged selection that extends into the torn edge and almost, but not quite, matches the shape of the edge, as shown in Figure 9.25.

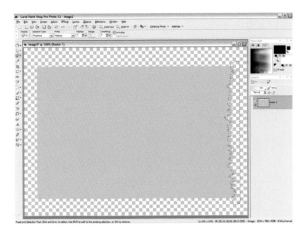

Figure 9.25

Make a new jagged selection within the torn edge.

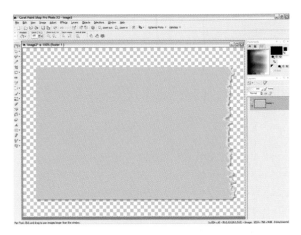

Figure 9.26

Simulated torn paper (with added drop shadow).

Reduce the saturation and increase the brightness of the selection, and then deselect. Optionally, you can roughen up the outside edge a bit with your image editor's Eraser tool or adjust the ragged line where the torn area and the untorn area meet using your Smudge tool. The result looks something like Figure 9.26, where a drop shadow was also added.

Enhancing the Edge

The lightened and desaturated part of the torn edge can be made to look more worn by adding a little noise and blurring it a bit. Other variations you can try are running a Soften brush along the part of the paper where the solid paper meets the tear, or running a warp tool or Smudge brush along the tear to make it even more irregular.

Mats and Frames

CREATING MATS AND FRAMES is much like creating a background. You begin just as you would for a background: open the image at the size you want, and then either choose a color and apply a texture or fill the image with a seamless pattern. What you do next depends on whether you want to plop your photo on top of a simple mat or make the photo appear as though it's placed behind a cutout in a frame.

Simple Mats

Create a rectangular image the size that you want for your mat. Fill with the color you want, and add a texture if you like. You might want to bevel the edges of the mat a bit, although this usually isn't necessary. In your layout, you can simply add a drop shadow to the mat to give it a 3D appearance. You should add your photo on a layer above the mat and add a slight drop shadow to the photo as well, to make it appear to lie on top of the mat.

Creating Cutouts for Frames

For a frame that lies on top of your photo, with the photo showing through a cutout in the frame, begin just as you do for a mat: create a rectangular image the size of your frame, fill with the color you want, and add a texture if you want your frame to be textured. Then to make the hole for the frame, use your selection tool to define a rectangular or elliptical selection within the frame, and delete the contents of the selection (see Figure 9.27).

Figure 9.27

A cutout made by deleting the contents of a selection.

Place the frame on a layer above your photo. Add a bevel to the frame using your image editor's beveling effect. Then add a drop shadow to the frame to make it look like it's lying above the background and the photo. The result is shown in Figure 9.28.

Figure 9.28

Example of a finished frame in use.

Fancier Mats and Frames

Not all mats and frames are rectangular. For oval mats and frames, use the same methods that you use for rectangular mats and frames, but start out with an oval rather than a rectangle. For really fancy mats and frames, start out with a piece of clip art or a character from a dingbat font set. To get 3D-looking frames, you can colorize and apply bevels to black-and-white clip art or dingbats, either alone or in combination with other shapes. A couple of examples are shown in Figure 9.29.

Figure 9.29

Frames made using clip art (left) and a dingbat (right). Clip art from Dover Publications' Art Nouveau Frames and Borders; dingbat from House of Lime DBL Corners.

Tags

NOW LET'S TAKE A LOOK at how to create simple rectangle-based tags. You can make a simple packing tag like the one in Figure 9.30 by first drawing a rectangle for the main body of the tag, and then drawing a smaller rectangle for the top of the tag. Use your image editor's shape-editing tool or Transform/Pick tool to shrink the top of the rectangle so that the sides angle in. If these shapes are on separate layers, merge the layers once you have the shapes lined up correctly. Then you only need to cut out a hole near the top of the tag, and add any texturing or shadowing that you want.

Figure 9.30

A simple packing tag.

You can make a rounded-top rectangular tag in much the same way: Draw a rectangle for the main body of the tag, and then draw a circle or ellipse for the top of the tag. Align these two shapes, merge the layers if the shapes are on separate layers, cut out a hole, and add a texture or shadowing if you like.

"Stamping" a Tag

You can add decorations to your tags using clip art or dingbat characters. For example, you can make simple clip art or dingbats look stamped onto your tag by adding the clip art or dingbat to its own layer, applying a texture to that layer, and reducing the layer opacity or using a blending mode, such as Multiply or Overlay, to blend the "stamp" onto the tag.

Metal-Rimmed Tags

You can create a metal-rimmed tag, like the one shown in Figure 9.31, by creating a round tag then adding a rim on its own layer. Step-by-step tutorials for making round metal-rimmed tags are included on the DVD.

Figure 9.31

A metal-rimmed tag.

Brads and Eyelets

RADS AND EYELETS are some of the easiest elements to make, especially if your image editor has a facility for creating 3D-looking spheres or rings, such as Paint Shop Pro's Balls and Bubbles effect and Magnifying Lens effect.

If your image editor doesn't have built-in 3D effects, you can still create some nice-looking brads and eyelets. Next, a general method for each is described, with specific methods for creating brads and eyelets in Paint Shop Pro and Photoshop Elements included on the DVD.

Image Size

In general, when creating brads and eyelets, start out with an image canvas of about half an inch by half an inch, set at the image resolution you normally use for your layouts. Be sure the background of the new image is transparent, and save the image as a PNG with transparency.

For a brad, create a circle centered in the image canvas. Fill it with a sunburst gradient with a highlight in the upper left and with highlights and shadows added with the Dodge and Burn tools, or use whatever means your image editor provides for simulating a 3D sphere.

For an eyelet, create a ring shape and add beveling to the ring, either with the Dodge and Burn tools or with a beveling effect if your image editor has one. If you can't make a ring directly, make a circle and then cut out a smaller, circular selection within the larger circle. Figure 9.32 shows a few examples of simple brads and eyelets.

Figure 9.32

Some simple brads and eyelets.

In addition to round brads and eyelets, you should try some other shapes as well. In any image editor, you can draw a shape and cut out a hole. Then you can add beveling shadows and highlights by hand or with a bevel effect if your image editor has a facility for adding bevels. As you'll see in the next chapter, another option for bevels is to use a plug-in filter, such as Bevel Boss, Glass, or Chrome, which are all included in Alien Skin Software's Eye Candy 5 Impact (a demo of which is included on the DVD). Figure 9.33 shows some examples of fancy brads and eyelets.

Fancy Brads and Eyelets

The shapes used for fancy brads and eyelets can also be made using clip art shapes or dingbat font characters. Copy and paste a clip art shape to its own layer or enter a character from a dingbat font, and then apply a bevel. (For font characters, first you may need to render the text—that is, convert it to raster—in order to apply a bevel or other effects.)

Figure 9.33

A few fancy brads and eyelets, created by Lauren Bavin.

Ribbons and Fibers

RIBBONS AND FIBERS add realistic dimension and texture to a layout, and it takes little effort to create them. Ribbons are basically patterned rectangles, and fibers are simply fancy lines.

Ribbons

Figure 9.34 shows a segment of basic gingham ribbon. To make such a ribbon, open a new image with a transparent background that's slightly taller than you want your ribbon to be. Add a rectangle that extends from the left side of the rectangle to the right. Fill the rectangle with a gingham pattern. Then on a new layer, add a thin solid-colored rectangle across the top of the patterned rectangle and on another new layer add a thin solid-colored rectangle across the bottom of the patterned rectangle (see Figure 9.35).

Add a slight bevel to each of the thin rectangles. Add a subtle drop shadow to each of these, making the shadow fall into the interior of the ribbon. Then merge the layers, and maybe add some shading. You can also give the ribbon a more natural look by merging the layers and then using your image editor's warping tools or applying a plug-in filter, such as Eye Candy's Jiggle or Xenofex 2's Flag.

Figure 9.34

Basic gingham ribbon.

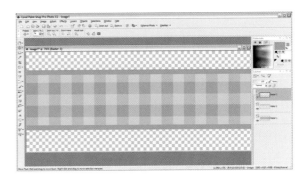

Figure 9.35

Add the ribbon's borders as long, thin rectangles on separate layers.

Figure 9.36 shows a grosgrain ribbon. This is made from a simple rectangle filled with a linear gradient with an angle of about 45°. Thin, vertical lines are then drawn along the width of the rectangle. To add edging, duplicate the original layer twice, and then use your Transform/Pick tool to shrink the height of each of the duplicate rectangles to get one thin rectangle along the top edge and one along the bottom edge. Merge the layers and add some shading.

Figure 9.36

A basic grosgrain ribbon.

Gingham and grosgrain ribbons are only two of the possibilities. For more ideas, take a look at Figure 9.37!

Figure 9.37

Sample ribbons and other fabric-like components (by Lauren Bavin) .

Creating Rick-Rack

It's easy to create rick-rack from a ribbon.

In Paint Shop Pro Photo, apply Effects > Distortion Effects > Wave to a ribbon. Set Amplitude for Horizontal Displacement to 0, and set Amplitude and Wavelength for Vertical Displacement to whatever values give you the results you want for your rick-rack.

In Photoshop Elements, apply Filter > Distort > Wave. Set Number of Generators to 1 and for Type select Sine. Leave the Scale settings at 100% and adjust Wavelength and Amplitude to give you the results you want.

Fibers

Just about any image editor has a paintbrush tool that can be tweaked for painting fancy lines. In addition to the basic round and square brush tips, you can choose more elaborate shapes. Some of these fancy brush tips are perfect for creating simulated fibers, such as cord or yarn.

Figure 9.38 shows an example of Paint Shop Pro's Twirly Star brush shape. On the left is a single dab of the brush, showing the shape of the brush tip itself. On the right is some yarn drawn with multiple back-and-forth drags of that brush, with Brush Variance settings that add some color variation and rotate the brush tip each time a dab is made.

Figure 9.38

Simulated yarn painted with a fancy brush tip.

You can get rather sophisticated effects if your image editor supports brush options that let you vary the brush's color, size, or rotation as you drag. For example, Paint Shop Pro has Brush Variance (available on the Brush Variance palette) and Photoshop Elements has More Options (available on the Brush Tool's options bar). Figure 9.39 shows a few examples of fibers created in Paint Shop Pro Photo X2 using different colors, brush shapes, and Brush Variance settings.

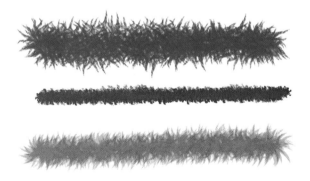

Figure 9.39

A few sample fibers.

Painting with Pictures

If your image editor has a tool that lets you paint with images—such as Paint Shop Pro's Picture Tubes—you can use these tools to make realistic-looking cords and ropes. Try spheres or clusters of spheres as the image with which you paint, setting the spacing quite low.

Figure 9.40 shows an example in which Paint Shop Pro's Rope Picture Tube is used to make a gold cord and tassel.

Figure 9.40

A cord and tassel made with Paint Shop Pro's Picture Tube tool.

Using and Creating Brushes

W E'VE JUST SEEN THAT YOU can
use brushes to create fibers, but there's
plenty more you can do with brushes.
You can use brushes to create background papers,
distress a paper or tag, or simulate a rubber stamp
effect. You can even create your own brushes for
personal use or to share.

Brushes for Paper Effects

Brushes are great for creating paper effects.
Consider the paper in Figure 9.41, for example.

This paper was made using the brush tips shown
in Figure 9.42, both of which are available in
Photoshop Elements. One brush was used to fill a
layer, and the other was used to add brush dabs
along the edges on a higher layer (with the blend
mode of the upper layer set to Soft Light).

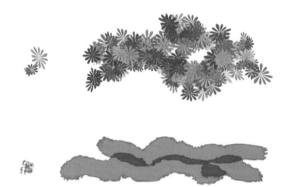

Figure 9.42

*The brushes used to create the paper: a Special Effects
brush and a Wet Media brush.*

To create these kinds of effects, open an image
that's the size and base color you want the paper
to be. Add a new layer and paint on that layer
with a brush of your choice, perhaps with brush
dynamics/variance enabled. Add another layer and
paint with a second brush, if you like. Continue in
this way until you get an effect that pleases you.
Remember that if you have separate layers, you
can adjust the opacity or blend mode of each layer
independently of the others. You can even blur one
or more of the layers or apply a special effect.

Figure 9.41

A paper created with brushes.

Grunge and Distressing Effects

Brushes can also be used to distress a paper, mat, or tag. Figure 9.43 shows a tag whose edges are being darkened with Photoshop Element's Burn tool, which utilizes brush tips. In this case, you select the tag or lock the layer's transparency, and then run the Burn brush run along the edges of the tag. This is an especially effective technique to use with a graphics tablet and stylus, with the brush size set to vary with the pressure applied when you paint with the stylus.

Distressing effects like this can be achieved with various grunge brushes, which have "dirty" or ragged brush tips, such as those shown in Figure 9.44.

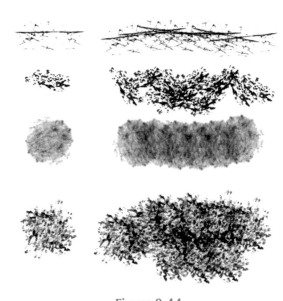

Figure 9.44

*Grunge brushes are useful for distressing paper
or other components.*

Use grunge brushes to paint colored smears and corrosive effects on your paper, or use them with your Burn brush to create burns and stains.

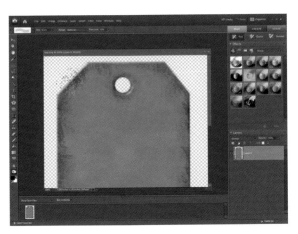

Figure 9.43

Distressing a tag with Photoshop Element's Burn tool.

Stamps

You can also use a brush like a rubber stamp. Suppose you have a brush that looks like a stylized vine, such as the one in Figure 9.45.

Figure 9.45

A vine-like brush tip.

You can use such a brush to "stamp" its image one or more times on a paper, tag, or other component. Figure 9.46 shows an example where the vine-like brush is stamped on textured paper.

Figure 9.46

The brush applied on a textured paper to create a stamping effect.

Figure 9.47 shows an example layout that features stamp-like brushes.

Figure 9.47

Layout featuring stamp-like brushes ("The Jhie Family" by Lie Fhung).

Creating Your Own Brushes

In most image editors, it's easy to create your own brush. Just open a new image with a white background and paint with black and gray, then export the image as a brush. White areas of the image will be transparent areas of your brush tip, black areas of the image will be fully opaque areas of your brush tip, and gray areas of the image will be semi-transparent areas of the brush tip. Figure 9.48 shows a few images appropriate for conversion to brush tips, and Figure 9.49 shows an example of the resulting brush tips put to use.

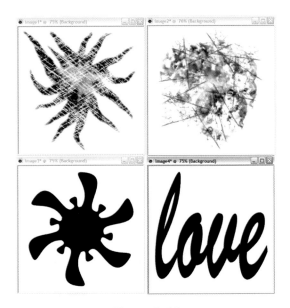

Figure 9.48

Examples of images that could be converted to custom brush tips.

Figure 9.49

The resulting brush tips put to use.

To export an image as a brush in Paint Shop Pro, choose File > Export > Custom Brush. This opens the dialog shown in Figure 9.50.

Figure 9.50

Create Brush Tip dialog in Paint Shop Pro Photo X2.

Maximum Brush Size

Be sure that the pixel dimensions of the image you use for creating a new brush don't exceed the maximum brush size limits for your image editor.

The limits are pretty liberal in today's image editors. In Paint Shop Pro Photo, the maximum size of a brush is 999 pixels × 999 pixels. In Photoshop Elements, the maximum brush size is 2500 pixels × 2500 pixels, large enough for you to create a brush that can fill a whole 12 × 12-inch page at 200 ppi! Keep in mind, though, that large brushes make serious demands on your computer's resources, so response time can be pretty slow.

Enter a name for your brush and a default Step (the spacing between dabs when you drag with the brush). If you like, you can also select Save Variance, which saves the current Brush Variance settings so that you can automatically load those settings when you load your brush tip. You also have the option of entering your name, copyright info, and a description of the brush. To create the brush, press OK. Your custom brush is then available in the brush tip selection list of any brush-like tool.

To export an image as a brush in Photoshop Elements, choose Edit > Define Brush. This opens the Brush Name dialog, shown in Figure 9.51.

Figure 9.51

Brush Name dialog in Photoshop Elements.

Enter a name for your brush, then click OK. The brush is added to the currently active brush library. When you switch to a new brush library, Photoshop Elements will ask whether you want to save the changes to the current brushes before switching to another library. If you want to save your brush in the current library, click Yes. Your brush will then be available for use with any brush-like tool. (If you choose No, your brush will not be saved.)

Brushes from Selections

You can also create a brush tip from a selection, which is a handy way to create a brush from a portion of a photo. In Paint Shop Pro, make your selection and then choose File > Export > Custom Brush. In Photoshop Elements, make your selection and then choose Edit > Define Brush from Selection.

Figure 9.52

"No Bunny" layout by Roberta D'Achille.

Time Flies

Cameron, it seems like it could have been yesterday that your Dad took the photo of you asleep in your basinette, and here you are nearly a teenager, what a wonderful young man you are turning into. My how time flies...

"Time Flies" layout by Lauren Bavin.

10

Enhancing Your Pages with Filters and Layer Styles

P ICTURE YOURSELF ADDING great text effects, modifying existing components, or creating your own sophisticated components. Whether you work from a scrapping kit or start from scratch, you can whip up whatever you need for your special layout. With filters and layer styles, you can create simply stunning effects in a snap.

Built-In Filters

ALL IMAGE EDITORS INCLUDE built-in filters. These may include filters that simulate the effects of physical camera filters or darkroom effects, such as blurring and sharpening, or they may produce special effects such as drop shadows, bevels, and artistic effects. You've already seen examples of several of both of these sorts of filters throughout the book.

Non-photo Uses of Photo Filters

Paint Shop Pro Photo's photographic filters are available in its Adjust menu (shown in Figure 10.1), and Photoshop Elements' photo filters are available in its Enhance menu (shown in Figure 10.2).

Figure 10.1

Paint Shop Pro Photo X2's Adjust menu.

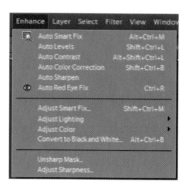

Figure 10.2

Photoshop Element 6.0's Enhance menu.

Some of these filters, although designed for adjusting photos, are also useful for graphics work. For example, filters for adjusting hue, lightness, and saturation can be used to alter the color of a background paper or scrapbook component, as shown in Figures 10.3 and 10.4.

Other photo filters that are also useful for graphics are those for blurring and sharpening. And noise reduction filters can be used to convert digital photos into paintings. If your image editor includes a Curves filter that allows you to modify the shape of the curve directly, you can even create some great metallic effects—just begin with a beveled gray figure and apply Curves, giving the curve an M- or W-like shape, as shown in Figure 10.5. You can then colorize the result using your favorite recoloring method to get a result like the one in Figure 10.6.

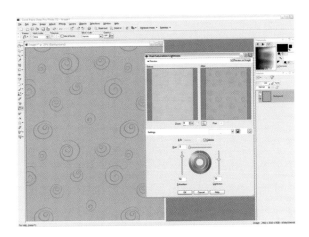

Figure 10.3

*Recoloring a background paper using Paint Shop
Pro Photo X2's Adjust > Hue and Saturation >
Hue/Saturation/Lightness adjustment.*

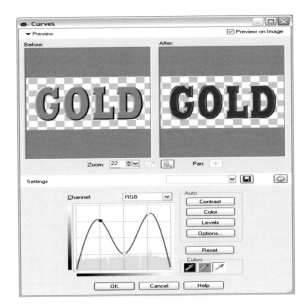

Figure 10.5

*Creating a metallic effect with Paint Shop Pro Photo's
Curves adjustment filter.*

Figure 10.4

*Recoloring a chrome picture frame with Photoshop Element 6.0's
Enhance > Adjust Color > Adjust Hue/Saturation.*

Figure 10.6

Add some color to get the metal of your choice.

Special Effects Filters

Special effect filters in Paint Shop Pro Photo are available in its Effects menu (shown in Figure 10.7), and Photoshop Elements' special effects filters are available in its Filter menu (shown in Figure 10.8).

Figure 10.7

Paint Shop Pro Photo X2's Effects menu.

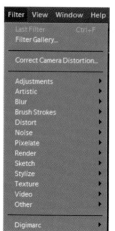

Figure 10.8

Photoshop Elements 6.0's Filter menu.

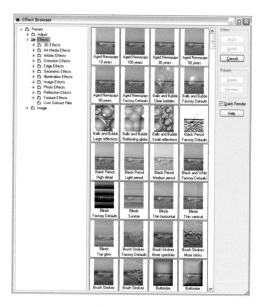

Figure 10.9

Paint Shop Pro X2's Effect Browser.

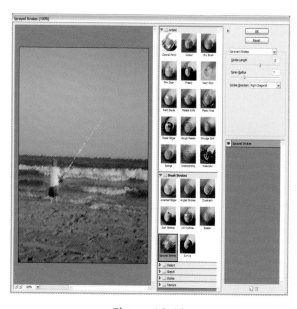

Figure 10.10

Photoshop Elements 6.0's Filter Gallery.

Most image editors include a way to browse all of its built-in effects. For example, Paint Shop Pro Photo X2 includes its Effect Browser (shown in Figure 10.9), and Photoshop Elements 6.0 includes its Filter Gallery (shown in Figure 10.10).

Paint Shop Pro users access the Effect Browser with Effects > Effect Browser. Photoshop Elements users access the Filter Gallery with Filter > Filter Gallery. The Filter Gallery can also be accessed by double-clicking the preview of a given effect in the Effects palette, shown in Figure 10.11.

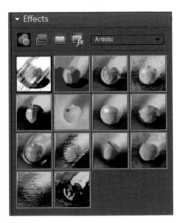

Figure 10.11

Photoshop Elements 6.0's Effects palette.

Examples of Paint Shop Pro Effects

Commonly used effects include Drop Shadow (Effects > 3D Effects > Drop Shadow), Inner Bevel (Effects > 3D Effects > Inner Bevel), and Texture (Effects > Texture Effects > Texture). The eyelet in Figure 10.12 was created using all three of these effects.

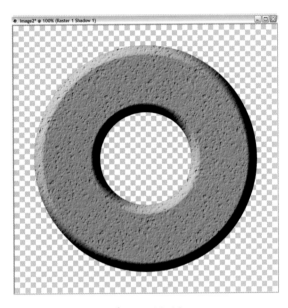

Figure 10.12

Eyelet made with Paint Shop Pro Photo X2's Drop Shadow, Inner Bevel, and Texture.

There are many other Paint Shop Pro built-in effects that scrappers are sure to use again and again. Let's take a look at a few.

Filter Limitations

Filters can be applied only on raster layers. If you have a vector shape or text that you want to apply a filter to, you'll first need to convert the shape or text to raster. In some image editors, converting to raster is called *simplifying* the layer or *rendering* the shape or text.

In addition, most filters can be applied only to grayscale images or 8-bit per channel color images. If your image has a color depth less than or greater than 8-bits per channel and you want all of your filters to be useable, you'll need to convert the image to 8-bits per channel.

Page Curl

When applied to a photo or mat, Page Curl creates a curled edge that resembles a book page in the process of being turned, often revealing another page or photo beneath. Paint Shop Pro Photo X2 has a Page Curl effect built in. To apply Page Curl, go to Effects > Image Effects > Page Curl. Figure 10.13 shows the Page Curl dialog box, with a corner of a photo curled and a transparent area revealed under the curl. You set the placement and radius of the curl and the color of the underside of the curled corner.

Figure 10.13

Paint Shop Pro Photo X2's Page Curl effect.

Transparency

To use the transparency setting in the Page Curl dialog box, the image must be on a true layer, not a background layer. This is true of any effect that includes a transparency setting.

Kaleidoscope

You can have a lot of fun experimenting with Paint Shop Pro's Kaleidoscope (Effect > Reflection Effects > Kaleidoscope). This effect creates a kaleidoscopic pattern from an image, as shown in Figure 10.14. You can use Kaleidoscope to create circular accents or fancy tiles.

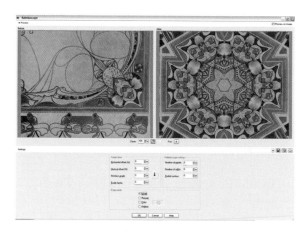

Figure 10.14

Paint Shop Pro Photo X2's Kaleidoscope effect.

Balls and Bubbles

For easy beads and brads, there's nothing like Balls and Bubbles (Effects > Artistic Effects > Balls and Bubbles). The interface is a little complex, with several different tabs in the dialog box, but it's definitely worth the effort of mastering. To help get you started, we've included some sample presets on the DVD.

You begin with a new image canvas that's a little larger than the size you want for the bead or brad and that has a transparent background. Using the bump map and environment map shown in Figure 10.15, you can get the result shown in the dialog box's right preview window.

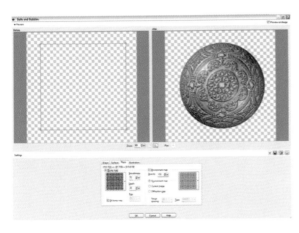

Figure 10.15

Paint Shop Pro Photo X2's Balls and Bubbles effect.

For a brad, take the result of Balls and Bubbles and flatten it a bit by applying Effects > Distortion Effects > Warp, as shown in Figure 10.16.

Figure 10.16

Warp flattens the ball to make a brad.

Other Effects

Those are only some of the Paint Shop Pro effects that are great for scrappers. Here are a few others to try:

- **Artistic Effects.** Chrome, Halftone, Hot Wax Coating, Magnifying Lens.

- **Distortion Effects.** Displacement Map, Pinch, Polar Coordinates, Punch, Twirl, Wave.

- **Image Effects.** Seamless Tiling.

- **Photo Effects.** Time Machine.

- **Reflection Effects.** Feedback, Pattern, Rotating Mirror.

- **Texture Effects.** Blinds, Fur, Mosaic – Antique, Mosaic – Glass, Sculpture, Tiles, Weave.

Examples of Photoshop Elements Effects

Photoshop Elements 6.0 provides many, many great artistic effects filters. For example, the Stamp filter (shown in Figure 10.17) produces a woodcut-like effect, and the Fresco filter (shown in Figure 10.18) produces a painting-like effect.

Most basic graphics effects that scrappers use, such as bevels and drop shadows, aren't made with filters in Photoshop Elements. Instead, these are made with layer styles, which you'll explore in the next section. But Photoshop Elements does include a few other graphics effect filters that are useful for creating background papers and scrapbooking components. One obvious candidate is the Texturizer filter and other filters in the Texture group, but let's look at a couple others that you might overlook.

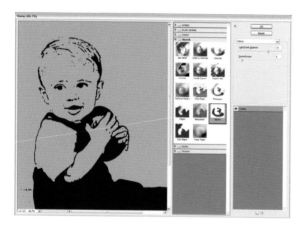

Figure 10.17

The Stamp filter creates a woodcut-like effect.

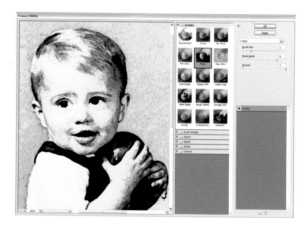

Figure 10.18

The Fresco filter is one of the many Photoshop filters that create painting-like effects.

Clouds

You can create some wonderful background papers beginning with Clouds (Filter > Render > Clouds). With Clouds, you set the background and foreground colors in Photoshop Elements' toolbox and then apply the filter. The result will look something like what's shown in Figure 10.19.

From there, there are all sorts of things you can do. One thing that's sure to produce some pleasing results is to apply one of the filters available under Filter > Texture. For example, Figure 10.20 shows the Texturizer being applied to the output of Clouds.

On a Cloud

In addition to the Texture filters, other filters that can give nice results when applied to the output of Clouds are several of the ones available under Sketch. The Note Paper, Torn Edges, and Water Paper filters all produce interesting papers when applied to the output of Clouds.

Figure 10.19

The Clouds filter is great for creating background papers.

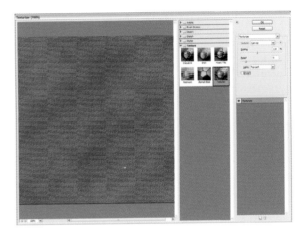

Figure 10.20

Give your Clouds-based paper some texture.

Polar Coordinates

Both Paint Shop Pro and Photoshop Elements include a Polar Coordinates filter. Polar Coordinates has two modes: one takes a circular object and maps it onto a rectangular plane, and the other takes a rectangular object and maps it onto a polar (circular) plane. The first mode probably isn't one you'll use very often, but you can get some very pleasing results using the second mode. For example, suppose you start out with a rectangular figure on a square canvas like the one shown in Figure 10.21.

You then apply Polar Coordinates with the Rectangular to Polar option selected. The result is a circular object like the one in Figure 10.22. What Polar Coordinates has done is transform the image into a version of itself that resembles a completely opened Chinese fan. What was at the top of the image is the center of the circle, and the two sides of the image now meet. What was at the bottom of the image now forms the outside edges of the resulting image.

You can use the result of Polar Coordinates as the basis for buttons or brads, or maybe even use the result as is for a circular sticker or stamp.

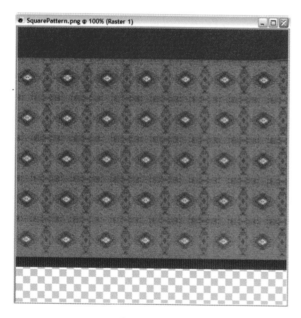

Figure 10.21

Begin with a rectangular object on a square image canvas.

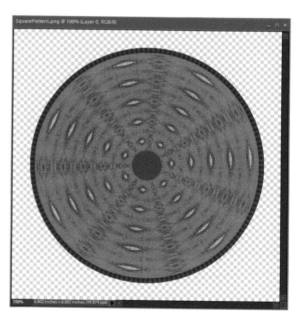

Figure 10.22

Polar Coordinates pulls and stretches the object into a circle.

Layer Styles

PHOTOSHOP, PHOTOSHOP ELEMENTS, and Paint Shop Pro Photo X2 all include a handy feature called *layer styles*. Layer styles produce effects like those made by special effects filters. However, layer styles have some advantages over filters. One big advantage is that a layer style is dynamic. When you change the content of a layer, any layer style associated with that layer conforms to the new content automatically. Let's look at an example.

Suppose you have some text on a layer. If you apply a beveling layer style to this layer, you'll get a result like what you see in Figure 10.23.

Figure 10.23

Beveling text with a layer style.

Edit the text on the layer and the bevel is applied immediately to any added text, as in Figure 10.24.

Figure 10.24

Layer styles conform to content that is added to the layer.

Another advantage of layer styles is that a layer style is editable, even in a later image editing session. For example, you could alter the look of the bevel in our text example, as in Figure 10.25.

Figure 10.25

You can alter the look at any time simply by changing the layer style settings.

Yet another advantage of layer styles is that they can be applied to vector layers as well as to raster layers.

Something from Nothing?

If you apply layer styles on an empty layer, all you'll see is an empty layer. But if you then paint onto the layer or add a shape or some text, the layer style will automatically be applied to the new layer contents.

Layer Styles in Paint Shop Pro

To access layer styles in Paint Shop Pro X2, you need to open a layer's Layer Properties dialog box, shown in Figure 10.26.

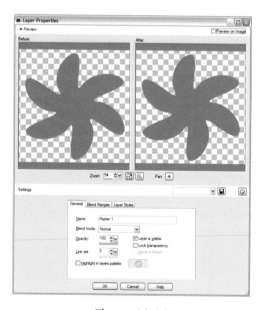

Figure 10.26

Layer Properties dialog box.

To open the Layer Properties dialog, do any of the following:

- Activate the layer you want to apply styles to and choose Layers > Properties.

- Right-click the layer's label on the Layers palette.

- Double-click the layer's label on the Layers palette.

After opening the Layer Properties dialog box, click the Layer Styles tab (see Figure 10.27).

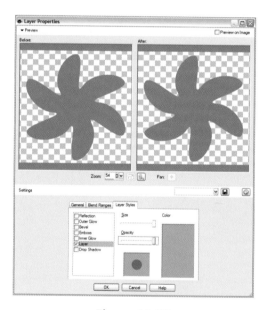

Figure 10.27

The layer style controls are on the Layer Styles tab.

There you see a list of checkboxes, one for each of the available layer styles and one labeled *Layer*, which refers to the actual image data on the layer. To activate a style, select its checkbox. To choose the settings for a particular style, highlight it by clicking its label, then choose the settings you want using the controls that appear to the right of the list of checkboxes. Figure 10.28 shows an example where Bevel, Inner Glow, and Layer are all activated, and where Bevel is highlighted. The Bevel controls are revealed, and you set these in order to specify the characteristics of the bevel.

To remove a layer style, deselect its checkbox. If you deselect the Layer checkbox, the layer's content becomes transparent and all that remains are the results of the layer styles. Figure 10.29 shows an example where Inner Glow and Outer Glow are selected but Layer is not.

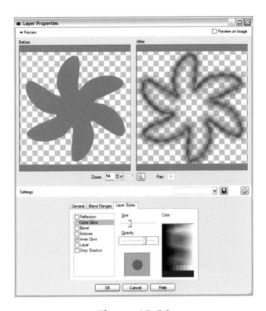

Figure 10.29

You can suppress the actual layer content, revealing only the result of the layer styles.

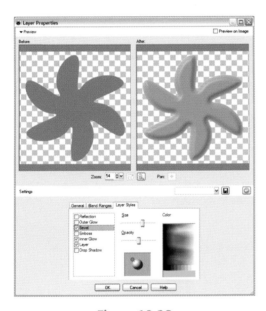

Figure 10.28

Controls for the Bevel layer style.

Layer Styles in Photoshop Elements

In Photoshop Elements, layer styles are added to a layer from the Effects palette (shown in Figure 10.30).

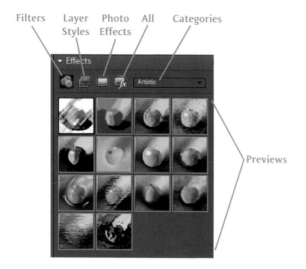

Figure 10.30

Photoshop Elements 6.0's Effects palette.

On the Effects palette, click the Layer Styles icon (the second one from the left), then choose the category of layer style that you'd like from the drop-down list, shown in Figure 10.31.

Figure 10.31

First, choose the category of layer style you want.

After you choose a category, the available styles in that category are displayed in the Effects palette. To apply a particular style, be sure that the layer you're interested in is activated, then do any one of the following:

- **In the Effects palette, click the preview of the style you want, and then click the Apply button.**

- **Drag the style you want from the Effects palette onto your image.**

- **Double-click the preview of the style you want.**

A layer that has a style applied to it will have a fancy *fx* on the right side of the layer's label in the Layers palette. To alter the settings of the style, double-click the *fx* or choose Layer > Layer Style > Style Settings. This opens the Layer Styles dialog box. Figure 10.32 shows a layer with several layer styles, along with the Style Settings dialog box. In this particular example, styles for Drop Shadow, Glow, and Bevel are all applied to the layer.

To remove all layer styles from a layer, make the layer active, and then choose Layer > Layer Style > Clear Layer Styles.

Figure 10.32

Change style settings in the Style Settings dialog box.

Plug-In Filters

A S YOU CAN SEE, it's possible to add interesting effects to your photos and scrapbook elements using built-in features of your image editor without adding anything else. However, there are lots of effects that can be produced better and faster, or with more features, using a plug-in filter.

Plug-in filters are helper applications that run within your image editor. These filters are sometimes referred to as *third-party plug-ins*, where *third-party* simply means that the plug-ins come from a company other than the company that developed your image editor. They provide additional functions to your image editor.

There are various types of plug-in filters. Here are some of those types, along with a few examples of commercial plug-ins that fall within each category:

- **Photo correction and enhancement.** Mystical Tint Tone and Color (Auto FX); ColorWasher and FocalBlade (The Plugin Site); Sharpener Pro (nik); Image Doctor and Exposure (Alien Skin Software); PixelCreation's ColorIntensity, TonalIntensity, and others (Twisiting Pixels).

- **Lighting effects.** Mystical Lighting (Auto FX); Shadow (Andromeda); Eye Candy 5 Impact's Perspective Shadow (Alien Skin Software).

- **Bevel and metallic effects.** Eye Candy 5 Impact's Bevel, Chrome, and Glass (Alien Skin Software); Super BladePro (Flaming Pear); DreamSuite Liquid Metal, Metal Mixer, and Dimension X (Auto FX).

- **Texture and pattern effects.** DreamSuite (Auto FX); HyperTyle (The Plugin Site); Plaid Lite (namesuppressed); Jama 3D and Lattice Composer (Redfield Plugins).

- **Natural and particle effects.** Xenofex 2's Lightning and Little Fluffy Clouds; KPT Effects (Corel); PixelCreation's Autocumulus, Constellation, and others (Twisting Pixels).

- **Special effects.** Puzzle Pro 2.0 and Page Curl 2.0 (AV Bros.); DreamSuite Series Two (Auto FX); Xenofex 2's Television; Raster Master (AmphiSoft).

- **Edge and Frame effects.** Photo/Graphic Edges 6.0 (Auto FX); Splat! (Alien Skin Software); Plugin Galaxy 2's Edges (The Plugin Site).

Plug-in or Stand-alone

There are also a few plug-ins that can run as stand-alone applications as well as running within an image editor. Filters from Auto FX (www.autofx.com) and Twisting Pixels (www.twistingpixels.com) are examples of this sort of dual-use filter.

Finding the Right Plug-In

Plug-ins come in freeware, shareware, and commercial versions. Some companies produce freeware versions of a plug-in, as well as a more advanced version with additional features that they market commercially. Some programmers write freeware plug-ins for the graphics community, asking nothing in return. Occasionally, plug-ins are *shareware*—free to test out and use, but if you like it and want to continue using it, you're honor-bound to compensate the developer.

Most commercial plug-ins have more extensive feature sets than do freeware, but some freeware filters are pretty powerful. Many commercial plug-ins also include additional resources, such as texture packs and light tiles; and they usually have distinctive and complex interfaces, which may not be an advantage if you don't like playing "hide and seek" with setting controls.

Many plug-ins make use of a handy feature called *presets.* Presets are saved settings combinations, which when loaded into the plug-in reproduce an effect previously constructed. For example, if you create a bluish metallic effect using Eye Candy 5 Impact's Chrome, you can save the settings that produce that effect as a preset and load it again any time in the future to quickly re-create that same effect. Exchanging presets with fellow users of your favorite plug-ins can be highly addictive. For example, the users of SuperBladePro by Flaming Pear Software have entire online communities devoted to the making and exchanging of presets.

What types of effects can you create with plug-ins? Any type you can conceive of and probably a few more! Bear in mind, if you have the knowledge, time, and patience, it's possible to create those effects using only the features of your image editor itself. But plug-ins provide shortcuts to effects that would be difficult or tedious to create manually.

On this book's resource DVD, you'll find many plug-in filter demos to try out and a few freebies as well. A word about demo versions—they come in several types, some of which are easier to work with than others. Demo versions are supplied by plug-in developers to allow you to test-drive the plug-ins. You can determine the quality of the effects as well as the functionality of the interface before you commit to a purchase.

Here are some demo version types you may come across, along with examples of plug-in demos of each type:

- **Time-limited, fully functional.** Alien Skin's Xenofex 2 is fully functional for 30 days. Alien Skin's Splat! is fully functional, except for the Picture Tube import/export feature.

- **Fuctionality-limited, but doesn't time out.** In some of the Twisting Pixels filter suites, a subset of the filters are fully functional.

- **Functional, but watermarks on finished image.** AV Bros. Page Curl and Puzzle Pro apply a watermark to images saved with the demo versions. The effects that aren't fully functional in the Twisting Pixels demos are also of this type.

- **Limits function to built-in images.** Auto FX plug-ins don't allow the use of your own images in the demo version. You can use all the functions of the plug-in, but you must use the images provided with the demo versions.

Freeware Plug-Ins

Do an Internet search for "freeware" and "plug-ins," and you'll find hundreds of links. However, there are a couple of sites that have already done the work for you, which makes it easy to find some excellent freeware plug-ins, in addition to commercial plug-ins. We recommend the following sites:

- **The Plugin Site.** www.thepluginsite.com offers its own commercial plug-ins, but that's not all. It also provides reviews in the Reviews section and a large number of links for both free and commercial plug-ins in the Resources section.

- **FreePhotoshop.com.** www.freephotoshop.com has hundreds of reviews and links for both free and commercial plug-ins, as well as other useful resources.

- **Graphicsoft at About.com.** http://graphicssoft.about.com/od/pluginsfiltersfree/ has lots of links to plug-ins, tutorials, and resources.

In Appendix A, "Resources," we also provide you with URLs to some of our favorite freebie filters.

Commercial Plug-Ins

There are thousands of commercial plug-ins available. Some are inexpensive: AmphiSoft, Redfield Plug-ins, and namesuppressed all offer great plug-ins at a very modest price. Some cost a bit more, and some even cost more than your image editor. We recommend trying demo versions of any commercial plug-in before you buy. Be sure the plug-in you're interested in will work properly with your image editor—contact the manufacturer if you are unsure—and that the plug-in creates effects you'll actually use.

Help!

Many commercial plug-ins come with extensive documentation, including built-in Help files, PDF manuals on the installation CD or available for download, and sometimes even paper manuals. Be sure to take a look at your plug-in documentation, the first place to look to find how to use your plug-in filters and how to troubleshoot if you run into any problems.

Don't Go Overboard

We aren't recommending that you purchase all of the commercial plug-ins we mention, of course. But you might want to give a few of them a look to see if you find a package or two that will come in handy for you in your digital scrapping projects.

You'll find a list of URLs to some of our favorite commercial filters in Appendix A.

Managing Your Plug-Ins

Plug-ins can be installed just as you would install any other application, either from a CD or, if you purchase online, from a downloaded installation file. Follow the manufacturer's instructions for installation.

It's a good idea to decide on how you'll organize your plug-ins before you actually install any. Since collecting plug-ins is just as addictive as collecting scrapbook elements, you could soon find yourself with a ton of software. If you would like to use the filters in more than one image editor, or if you want to limit the amount of uninstalling and reinstalling you might have to do in the future, it's a good idea to use a single plug-ins folder that is *not* contained within the Programs folder of any image editor. That way, if you have to uninstall or upgrade an image editor, you won't have to reinstall the plug-ins. Putting a folder in My Documents is a good idea. You can then set up subfolders inside that main plug-ins folder to organize plug-ins from various developers.

Some plug-ins will automatically detect the image editors on your computer and will try to install to one or more of those applications' Program folder. You can override this by choosing a custom installation or by clicking on the Browse button to change the installation folder.

Occasionally you'll find that a plug-in doesn't work or work properly within your image editor. If you receive an error message that the plug-in isn't correctly configured, the most common cause is a corrupt version of a necessary DLL file. The simple solution is to download and install the correct version, which Sally has available at www.dizteq.com/joestuff/freestuff.html.

You may need to copy the DLL to the Windows > System folder, the Windows > System 32 folder, or the program folder of the image editor you're using. If in doubt, install it in all three.

Once you have a plug-in installed, you need to tell your image editor where to find it:

- **Paint Shop Pro Photo X2.** Go to File > Preferences > File Locations (see Figure 10.33). In the File Types pane, click Plug-Ins. In the right panel, click the Add button to add a new folder location, and then the Browse button to browse to the plug-ins folder you'll use. You can have as many plug-ins folders as you like, so if you don't want to load all your plug-ins all of the time, you can configure the folder path in this Preference setting quickly. To access the plug-ins, go to Effects > Plugins. Click the menu entry for the plug-in you want, and the plug-in interface will open.

- **Photoshop Elements 6.0.** Go to Edit > Preferences > Plug-Ins to open the Preferences dialog (see Figure 10.34). Check the box to enable Additional Plug-Ins Folder, click the Choose button, and browse to your plug-ins folder. You'll then be able to access plug-ins installed in the Plug-ins subfolder inside the Program folder for Photoshop Elements 6.0 and those installed in your additional plug-ins folder. To access the plug-ins, go to the Filter menu, and the plug-in names will appear at the bottom of the list. Click the name for the plug-in you want, and its interface will open.

Figure 10.33

Paint Shop Pro Photo X2's File Locations dialog box.

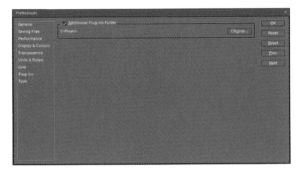

Figure 10.34

Photoshop Elements 6.0's Preferences dialog.

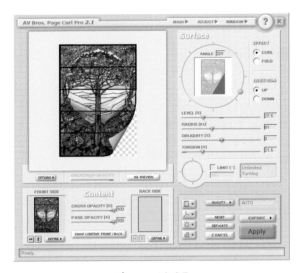

Figure 10.35

Page Curl 2.0 creates page curls, of course.

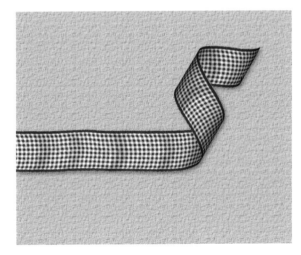

Figure 10.36

But it also curls ribbons—and a lot more.

Some Plug-In Examples

Let's take a brief look at some of the filters we've mentioned. Demos of these filters and others are provided on the resource DVD.

AV Bros. Plug-Ins

Among the products from AV Bros. are two marvelous special effects filters: Puzzle Pro and Page Curl 2.0. As the names suggest, with Puzzle Pro you can create simulated jigsaw puzzles, and with Page Curl 2.0 you can simulate a page in the process of being turned. Page Curl 2.0 provides a lot more functionality than a typical page curl filter, however. Sure you can create a page curl, as in Figure 10.35. But you can also create all kinds of folds and curls. For example, Figure 10.36 shows a ribbon that was curled with Page Curl 2.0.

Alien Skin Plug-Ins

Alien Skin Software (www.alienskin.com) makes some of the best plug-ins for digital scrapbookers. Alien Skin plug-ins come with an actual paper manual to guide you, as well as many presets to get you started. Here are a few of their filter packages that are of particular interest to scrappers:

- ⦿ **Eye Candy 5 Impact.** Suite of ten filter effects, including Bevel, Chrome, Glass, and Perspective Shadow.

- ⦿ **Eye Candy 5 Textures.** Ten filter effects, including updated versions of some of the effects from the older Eye Candy 4000 filter set (Animal Fur, Marble, Swirl, Texture Noise, Weave, and Wood) and four new filters (Brick Wall, Diamond Plate, Reptile Skin, and Stone Wall).

- ⦿ **Xenofex 2.** Fourteen filter effects, including Constellation, Flag, Lightning, Puzzle, and Rip Open. Some filters particularly good for scrapbooking are Stain, Cracks, Crumple, and Burnt Edges.

- ⦿ **Splat!** An excellent choice for scrapbookers. The six effects in this package are Fill Stamp, Border Stamp, Patchwork, Resurface, Edges, and Frames.

Xenofex 2 and Splat! feature some filter effects that are "most wanted" by digital scrapbookers. Xenofex 2 can simulate crumpled paper effects and torn, burned, ripped edges. Splat! has numerous edge and frame effects that are simple to use and customize. To give you an idea of what the possibilities are, take a look at the layouts in Figures 10.37 through 10.39.

Figure 10.37

"Backyard Blooms" layout by Sally Beacham (photo courtesy of Ron Lacey). Filters used are Splat's! Resurface and Frame filters.

Figure 10.38

"Renee & Jason" layout by Sally Beacham. Page layout kit from Angela M. Cable, using filters from Eye Candy 4000 (the precursor of the Eye Candy 5 series).

Figure 10.39

"Autumn Walk" layout by Lori J. Davis. Filters used are from Splat! (Border Stamp, Edges, and Resurface), Xenofex 2 (Little Fluffy Clouds), Eye Candy 5 Textures (Texture Noise), and Eye Candy 5 Impact (Chrome and Perspective Shadow).

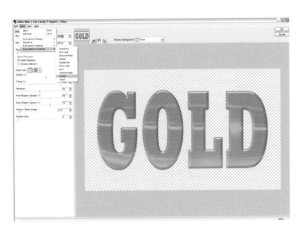

Figure 10.40

Alien Skin's Eye Candy 5 interface, with the Glass filter active and Filter menu open.

Swapping Filters

Most of the Alien Skin line of plug-ins use a uniform interface from which you can access any of the Alien Skin filters that share that interface—even filters from separate suites. That's certainly a convenient feature! If you don't like one filter's effects, you can just try another one without first having to exit the plug-in's dialog box. Figure 10.40 shows a dialog box with the Eye Candy 5 Impact Glass filter active and the Filter menu open.

For beautiful buttons, beads, brads, and eyelets, you can hardly beat the Bevel, Chrome, and Glass effects of Eye Candy 5 Impact. And as demonstrated in Figure 10.41, these filters are also excellent for enhancing text.

Figure 10.41

Bevel, Chrome, and Glass are great for enhancing text.

Twisting Pixels

In addition to two collections of art media effects—ArtStudio Pro Volume 1 and ArtStudio Pro Volume 2—Twisting Pixels offers packages of fantastic graphics effects that any scrapper would love:

- ⊙ **PixelCreation. Nineteen visual effects and tone enhancement filters. These are particularly good for adding a new sky to a photo or creating some starry text.**

- ⊙ **PixelPaper. Fifteen realistic paper effects, including Bend, Border, Burn, Crinkle, Crumple, Curl, Edge, Fold, and Rip.**

- ⊙ **PixelPack. Ten special effects filters. In addition to beveling and texturizing filters, there are some unusual finds here, such as LabelMaker and PostageStamp.**

These three suites of graphics effects are available individually or bundled together as the PixelCreationBundle. To get an idea of what you can do with these filters, take a look at Figure 10.42, where a crumpled envelope is made with PixelPack's PostageStamp and PixelPaper's Crumple.

Figure 10.42

A crumpled envelope made with Twisting Pixels filters.

The PixelPack filters include controls for adding reflections and bumps to surfaces. Like Paint Shop Pro's Balls and Bubbles and the beveling filters in Alien Skin's Eye Candy 5 Impact, the filters enable you to use environment/reflection maps (called Surface in the Twisting Pixels interface). And like Paint Shop Pro's Balls and Bubbles, the PixelPack filters also give you the option of adding a bump map. Figure 10.43 shows an example using the RockCandy filter.

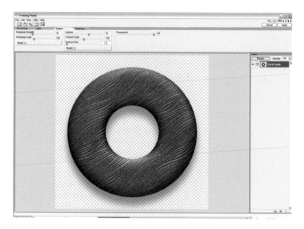

Figure 10.43

PixelPack can add bumps and reflections to your shapes and text.

A powerful feature of all Twisting Pixels plug-ins is the ability to apply multiple filters at once, layering the filter effects one above the other (see Figure 10.44). You can add new effect layers, selectively turn individual layers on and off, change the order of the layers, or activate a particular layer and tweak the settings of the filter applied there.

One of the features that characterize most of The Plugin Site filters is that the interface includes several modes. For example, Plugin Galaxy 2 includes a Novice mode, which simply lists the presets available for the various filters in the Plugin Galaxy suite. As you can see in Figure 10.45, this mode is very simple and friendly.

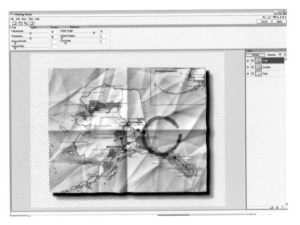

Figure 10.44

Apply multiple filters all at once with layering.

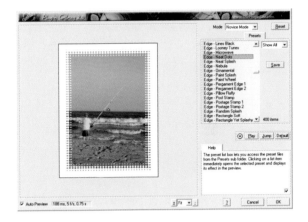

Figure 10.45

Plugin Galaxy's Novice mode is simple and unintimidating.

The Plugin Site

The Plugin Site is a great source of information on plug-ins and a catalog of much of what's available in the world of plug-ins. In addition, The Plugin Site offers its own line of handy plug-ins. Among these are the several members of the Photo Wiz family—filters for correcting and enhancing your photos. These include ColorWasher, FocalBlade, and Black & White Styler. There are also a host of special effects filters, and among these is the latest addition to The Plugin Site offerings: Plugin Galaxy 2.

Compare this with the Expert mode, shown in Figure 10.46. This mode gives the hands-on user about as much control as you can imagine!

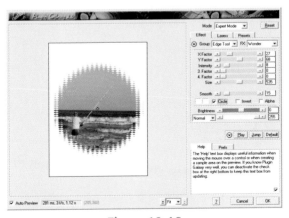

Figure 10.46

Expert mode gives you all the control you could want.

Did you notice the Layers tab in the Expert mode interface? Like the Twisting Pixels suites, Plugin Galaxy enables you to apply multiple filters in a single shot, layering filter effects one on top of another. Figure 10.47 shows the Layers tab for a multiple-filter effect.

Figure 10.47

You can layer multiple filters to create complex effects.

Plug-In Shopping Tips

At this point, you may be wondering where to begin. There are so many plug-ins, and you have limited time and funds. So before you head out plug-in shopping, be sure to explore the power of your image editor. Get familiar with your image editor's built-in filters and, if available, layer styles. You don't want to spend money on filters that duplicate what can already be done in your image editor.

When you do decide to go shopping for plug-ins, have in mind the sorts of features you want, and see if the plug-ins you're considering actually have those features. As we mentioned earlier, try out the demo or trial version of any commercial plug-in that is on your list to be sure that the plug-in is compatible with your image editor and that it provides the functionality you need. And if a freeware plug-in does everything that you want, put away your wallet and download the freebie.

Most of all, once you've acquired your plug-ins, enjoy yourself! Plug-ins aren't simply tools to help get your work done—they're also loads of fun.

Part IV
Scrapbook Inspiration

"Designer Appliance" layout by Lauren Bavin.

Theodore Beckett Stoup
gentleman of leisure
man about town
fashion plate
ladies' man

What a little man!
You've been all boy
from the day
you stepped into
my heart.

December 2006

11

Inspiration

PICTURE YOURSELF SITTING DOWN with all the tools and resources you've discovered so far in this book. You've got photos, software, and digital elements. And then—you're stuck. How to combine them to create a page, album, or hybrid project? If you need inspiration, use this chapter as a guide. Feel free to shamelessly *scraplift* ideas for layout schemes, design themes, color harmonies, and journaling.

Scraplifting is the concept of using other scrapbook layouts as thought starters. It's the highest form of flattery in the scrapbook world—to have your layout scraplifted by other scrapbookers, especially when they give you credit for the idea! So feel free to share and utilize the ideas you see here. All the layouts you'll see in this section were created with the digital resources you'll find on the book's DVD, so you can recreate them as closely as possible if you like. Or, use them as thought-starters, and create your own unique version.

Color My World

FOR ANY DIGITAL SCRAPBOOKER, a technique to learn well is how to re-color a digital element. One of the greatest advantages of digital scrapbooking is that you'll *always* have paper and embellishments to match any photo or existing layout. A gold eyelet doesn't have to be gold for long! The layout pictured in Figure 11.1 uses components from Terry Maruca's Wedding kit and Doris Castle's Pink Magic kit, both of which can be found on this book's resource DVD. The gold mesh was originally dark gray, the spatter dots pink, the ribbon green—in fact, the only component that has not been re-colored is the film frame!

Figure 11.1

"Dream Future" layout by Sally Beacham.
Scrapbook components from Terry Maruca's Wedding
kit and Doris Castle's Pink Magic kit.

To demonstrate how easy this can be, open an image from the DVD collection of goodies. You can choose any element you want from the various kits on the DVD, but a gray alpha letter in Roberta D'Achille's Pappy's Flannels kit is used here. The background of this alpha letter is a medium-gray, which makes it a good candidate to colorize. Many applications have specialized tools for correcting color, but we'll go the simple route.

Most full-featured image-editing applications have a means to change color, or *colorize*, by modifying an existing color's hue, saturation, or lightness values:

- **Paint Shop Pro Photo X2.** Go to Adjust > Hue and Saturation > Colorize. Move the sliders to adjust the hue and saturation values. Check the Preview on Image box to see the change updated on the image as well as in the Preview pane on the right side.

- **Photoshop Elements 5.0 and 6.0.** In Full Edit mode, go to Enhance > Adjust Color > Hue/Saturation. Check the Colorize and Preview boxes. Move the Hue, Saturation, and Lightness sliders to change the color of the image.

The colored alpha letters in Figure 11.2 are all created from that single gray alpha letter. To change a color, adjust the Hue slider. To make the color brighter, increase the Saturation value. Decreasing the Saturation value adds more gray to the color—if you slide the Saturation slider to its lowest value (0 in Paint Shop Pro, –100 in Elements), the image will be completely de-saturated, and thus gray. Use the Lightness slider to make the color lighter or darker.

Out, Out, Darned Black!

You'll soon discover that it's difficult, if not impossible, to colorize pure black or pure white. That's because (digitally, at least!) black is the absence of ALL color, and white is the presence of ALL color. Our methods of re-colorizing work best on colors or shades of gray. If you want to re-color an element which is pure black, lighten it to a shade of gray. You'll need to darken a white element. This is the reason we showed you how to colorize using a gray button in Figure 11.2. You will notice that the black letter on the tile doesn't change even though the surrounding tile does.

Figure 11.2

Alpha letters re-colored by adjusting Hue, Saturation, and Lightness values.

There are other tools to selectively re-color elements. In each application, look for features or tools that modify hue, saturation, lightness, tint, color balance, color cast, or features that remove or replace colors.

You can re-color portions of elements by selecting the area you want colored. In Figure 11.3, the pearl embellishment was originally white with a blue bead in the center. The white beads were re-colored yellow, but the blue bead remained blue. This was accomplished by creating a circular selection around the blue bead, inverting the selection so that the blue bead was the only portion NOT selected, and colorizing the white beads to yellow.

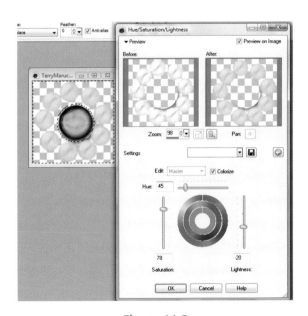

Figure 11.3

Pearl embellishment from Terry Maruca's Wedding Kit selectively re-colored.

Layouts

ARMED WITH THE TOOLS and features you've learned about previously in this book, you are ready to start creating your own layouts. In the next section, you'll see layouts created from several of the kits found on the book's resource DVD.

Doris Castle's Legacy of Heritage Kit

Doris Castle has created a beautiful kit full of antique- and vintage-style elements. There are several Quick Pages, shown in Figure 11.4, if you'd like to create something quickly, and a variety of papers and embellishments, if you'd like to build your own layouts.

Figure 11.4

Quick Pages from Doris Castle's Legacy of Heritage kit, from this book's resource DVD.

So let's see what some members of Doris's creative team have done with her kit.

Erica Nunez created a beautiful heritage layout, shown in Figure 11.5, by layering a brown paper with a ripped edge over the newsprint papers from the kit (notice how she's turned the newsprint sideways). The black-and-white photo has been framed and a photo edge overlay added. A photo embellishment is tucked between two layers of newsprint—simply layer the images in the Layers palette stack, and use the Mover tool to position them as you like.

Figure 11.5

"Elsa Nunez" layout by Erica Nunez, from Doris Castle's Legacy of Heritage kit.

Figure 11.6 and 11.7 show a hybrid project created from the same kit, by Corinna Stevens. It's a richly embellished wedding album, with printed components from the kit combined with scrapbook items purchased from a craft store. It's hard to distinguish the digital elements from the real ones!

Doris's creative team members Michelle Bowley, Kaitlynn Gonzalez, Teri-Lynn Masters, Trish Richhart, Inda Permata Sari, and Lizzy Wurmann created the layouts seen in Figure 11.8—all from the same kit. Some of the layouts use vintage photographs, and others use more current photos, some of them colorized to appear aged.

Figure 11.6

Album by Corinna Stevens, from Doris Castle's Legacy of Heritage kit.

Figure 11.7

Open view of album by Corinna Stevens, from Doris Castle's Legacy of Heritage kit.

Figure 11.8

Layouts created from Doris Castle's Legacy of Heritage kit.

Lauren Bavin's World Traveler Kit

Lauren Bavin, head designer at www.digitalscrap-bookplace.com, created a kit perfect for vacation photos (see Figure 11.9). This kit also includes a great Quick Page, which was used to create the lead illustration in Chapter 3 of this book.

Tara Dreier used the kit to create a scrapbook page in remembrance of a family vacation (see Figure 11.10).

Some interesting features of this layout:

- The text and brads are aligned to curve with the circular arrow.

- The photos are all placed on an angle. Don't keep all your photos centered and straight, add some interest by using offset placement and angled orientation.

- It's okay to position photos and objects so that part of the object is outside the image (and thus will appear to be cut off at the edge of the image).

- Tara used two alpha letter tiles from Lauren Bavin's Embossed Tab Alpha set, which is found on the resource DVD, to create the two-letter state abbreviation for Arizona!

- If you like the look of a multi-photo layout, you can crop portions from the main focal image and resize them to use in film-strip frames.

Figure 11.9

World Traveler layout kit by Lauren Bavin, on this book's resource DVD.

Figure 11.10

"Arizona" layout by Tara Dreier, using Lauren Bavin's World Traveler kit.

Penny Manning, Sharon Reus, Jenni Bader, Paula O'Neill, and Lauren Bavin created their own variations from the World Traveler kit or Quick Page, all shown in Figure 11.11.

Notice how each designer has used the kit elements in different ways. Components are re-sized, positioned above or below photos, and used vertically or horizontally. The kit can also be used for vintage or antique photos. Never limit yourself to the designer's vision—use your own!

Figure 11.11

Layouts using World Traveler kit by Lauren Bavin, on this book's resource DVD.

Glenda Ketcham's Feminine Heritage Kit

Here's an example of scrapbook components that were created to complement a specific photograph. The layout kit in Figure 11.12 was created by Glenda Ketcham and inspired by a hand-tinted wedding photo from the 1940s. The layout in Figure 11.12 is the result of a collaboration between scrapbooker and designer!

Some techniques from this layout that you might like to try:

- One letter of the title is created as a large drop cap initial with the Text Tool of the image editor. Then, digital "buttons" are added over the initial to add some texture and interest.

- Sometimes antique or vintage photos have physical damage that's too difficult or time-consuming to repair. Occasionally, that damage can be concealed by the positioning of the photo and scrapbook components. In this case, there is significant damage to the portion of the photo that is hidden by the pinned ribbon and the flowers in the bottom-right corner!

- Digital photos (or high-resolution scans of film photos) can be created at larger sizes than you might normally work with in a paper scrapbook layout. So don't be afraid to work with large photos, and layer elements over the edges to create balance in the composition.

- Create more complex digital embellishments by combining them. In Figure 11.13, the bow and tag embellishment was created from four separate components in the scrapbook kit.

Figure 11.12

Feminine Heritage layout kit by Glenda Ketcham, on this book's resource DVD.

Figure 11.13

"Beacham Wedding" layout by Sally Beacham, from kit components by Glenda Ketcham.

Lori Lindsey, Chris Hutchings, and Glenda Ketcham created their own versions with the Feminine Heritage Kit, shown in Figure 11.14. Chris Hutchings used the focal photo as background paper, adding the scrapbook elements around the edges to create a layout that combines both graphics-style and faux-realistic techniques.

Figure 11.14

Layout variations from the Feminine Heritage kit components by Glenda Ketcham.

Roberta D'Achille's Pappy's Flannels Kit

It's not difficult to find "girly" layout kits and components, but sometimes locating scrapbook kits that work for masculine themes requires some research (or creating your own!). The Pappy's Flannels kit, in Figure 11.15, by Roberta D'Achille (on this book's resource DVD) can be used to create boyishly good-looking layouts; and it is versatile enough to use for many other occasions. The background papers and elements in this kit are heavily textured to represent menswear fabrics, such as wool, suede, and leather.

Ramona Vaughn used the Pappy's Flannels kit to create her "Froggin" layout, shown in Figure 11.16. This layout features a lot of journaling. Notice the positioning of the elements around the text, creating a frame effect. Also, Ramona has cropped the photo frame so that it fits two photos, and she's turned it to a vertical orientation.

Ramona Vaughn and Sally Beacham created additional layouts with the Pappy's Flannels kit. In Figure 11.17, notice that the bottom layout is done almost entirely in shades of gray. Layouts don't have to be colorful to have impact!

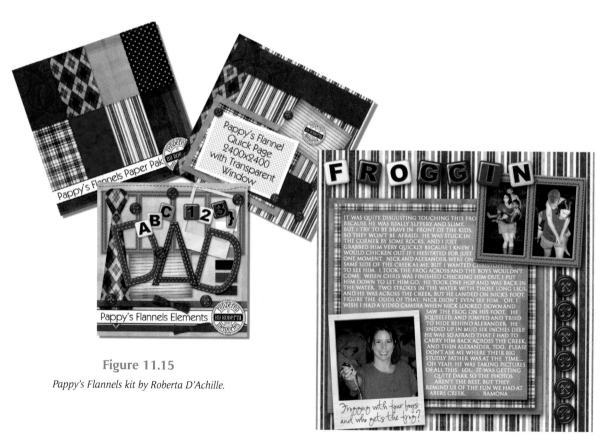

Figure 11.15

Pappy's Flannels kit by Roberta D'Achille.

Figure 11.16

"Froggin" layout by Ramona Vaughn, using components from Roberta D'Achille's Pappy's Flannels kit.

228

Figure 11.17

Layouts using Roberta D'Achille's Pappy's Flannels kit.

Figure 11.18 shows a layout created from the Pappy's Flannels kit, with additional elements from Angela Cable's Winter Holidays kit, also on the book's DVD. The elements from the Pappy's Flannels kit were colorized to coordinate with the little boy's shirt. A circular cutout was created in a full-size background paper (also colorized), and the frame elements and photos were layered under it. Another technique you might like to try—blue buttons from Angela's kit were substituted for the letter "O," and a charm for the letter "L," in the word "cool." You can take whatever creative license you like—substitute objects for letters, turn objects upside-down or sideways, crop, resize, or re-color them.

Figure 11.18

"Cool Dude" layout by Sally Beacham, with kit components from Roberta D'Achille and Angela Cable.

Lie Fhung's Painting Kit

Lie Fhung has created a painting-themed kit, with elements like wooden frames, buckles, tapes, clips, paint splotches, and other related items. The elements in this kit, shown in Figure 11.19, are versatile enough to be combined easily with other kits. The painting theme can be used for many types of photos.

There are also two Quick Pages included with the kit (see Figure 11.20). These can be rotated or flipped to give each page a different orientation, and you can add additional elements to further personalize them.

Jeannette Mulligan created a layout from the Painting kit, shown in Figure 11.21.

Jeannette Mulligan, Novita Solihin, Sally Beacham, and Lie Fhung produced variations on a theme with the Painting kit, seen in Figure 11.22, including a greeting card seen earlier in Chapter 4. The wooden frame has been used in several sizes and orientations, and the gold-embossed spatter circle has been used as a backing element and frame highlight.

Figure 11.20

Painting kit Quick Pages by Lie Fhung, on this book's resource DVD.

Figure 11.19

Painting kit by Lie Fhung, on this book's resource DVD.

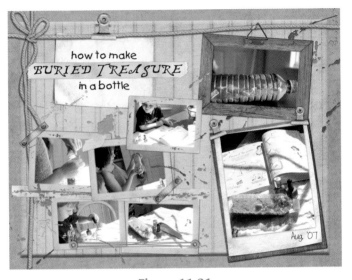

Figure 11.21

"Buried Treasure" layout by Jeannette Mulligan, using components from Lie Fhung's Painting kit.

Some unusual techniques used in the layout from Figure 11.21:

- The title was created by placing the middle line of text on a separate element, placed over a journaling square printed with the top and bottom lines.

- Jeannette visually attached items to the string border, and then attached other items to the attachments! Use layers, the Eraser Tool, and shadows to create realistic objects in your layouts.

- You might not normally use a photo that cuts off the top of a subject's head or that focuses on just a body part. But when used in a group on a layout, these types of photos can tell the story just as well as a perfectly framed and posed photo.

Figure 11.22

Layout variations using Lie Fhung's Painting kit.

Glenda Ketcham's Let's Play Kit

Glenda created a fanciful kit full of toys, denim, bandana prints, and eyelet lace to suit almost any children's layout. (See Figure 11.23.) In fact, the "Dedication" layout at the beginning of this book uses this kit.

Chris Hutchings created the layout shown in Figure 11.24 from Glenda's Let's Play kit. She used three photos of equal size to tell the story, but staggered them across the width of the layout. She also created a visual triangle with three teddy-bear "stickers" that lead the eye to the central photo.

Figure 11.24

"Journey" layout by Chris Hutchings, from the Let's Play kit.

Figure 11.23

Let's Play kit by Glenda Ketcham, on this book's resource DVD.

Shawn Walter created the simple layout in Figure 11.25 that places emphasis on the photos yet tells the story in a unique way. There are three photos of unequal sizes, but they are all simply framed, with a white border, and then aligned to create a perfect visual rectangle. Shawn used a handwriting font to add the title directly on the largest photo. Shawn also used a staple to attach the wire and tag to the layout.

Lori Linsey, Chris Hutchings, and Glenda Ketcham also created layouts using the Let's Play kit, as seen in Figure 11.26. The primary color scheme of this kit works with many photos.

Figure 11.25

"Climb, Baby, Climb" layout by Shawn Walter, from Glenda Ketcham's Let's Play kit.

Figure 11.26

Layout variations using Glenda Ketcham's Let's Play kit.

Roberta D'Achille's Baseball Season Kit

Sports themes are very popular scrapbooking subjects. Roberta D'Achille created a baseball-themed kit that will work for heritage photos, too. (See Figure 11.27.)

Ramona Vaughn created the layouts shown in Figures 11.28 and 11.29 using the Baseball Season kit. It's not so coincidental the kit's color scheme matches Ramona's sons uniforms—Auntie Roberta is the designer! This is another happy collaboration between designer and scrapbooker.

Notice that while both layouts are similar in color scheme, they differ in style. Figure 11.28 shows a graphic-style layout, with the photos layered in a montage in the layout. Figure 11.29 is a more traditional realistic-style layout, although Ramona has incorporated a graphics photo technique by masking away some of the photo background in the bottom right corner.

Kaitlynn Gonzalez used the Baseball Season kit to create a vintage-style layout that is still baseball-themed, shown in Figure 11.30. Substitute non-sports themed elements for the baseball components, and this layout could work for nearly any type of photo. Another interesting technique Kaitlynn has employed is to use the baseball stitching to frame a journaling box.

Figure 11.27

"Baseball Season" by Roberta D'Achille, on this book's resource DVD.

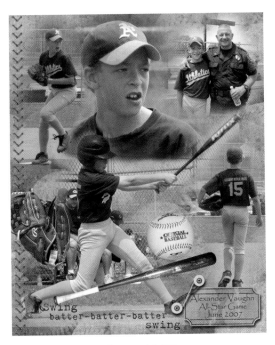

Figure 11.28

"Alexander Vaughn, All-Star Game" layout by Ramona Vaughn, from Roberta D'Achilles Baseball Season kit.

Figure 11.29

"Nick's First Season" layout by Ramona Vaughn, from Roberta D'Achilles Baseball Season kit.

Figure 11.30

"First Baseball Game" layout by Kaitlynn Gonzalez, from Roberta D'Achilles Baseball Season kit.

Perhaps your baseball loyalties lie with a team of different colors. No problem—re-color the components to match your favorite team colors. Whether you are a fan of the Boston Red Sox, Toronto Blue Jays, Yokohama BayStars, college, high school, or Little League teams, you can re-color elements within the kit to work with your photos. And don't forget you can use these elements for other types of layouts, too, not just sports-themed ones. In Figure 11.31, you can see papers and elements from the Baseball Season kit re-colored to match several teams' colors.

Figure 11.31

Components from Baseball Season kit re-colored to match team colors.

Doris Castle's Pink Magic Kit

The Pink Magic kit by Doris Castle (shown in Figure 11.32) is a very pretty feminine theme. It can be used as is to create layouts for weddings, birthdays, baby showers, proms—lots of special occasions. The kit works well with antique photos, too.

Denise Doupnik created two greeting cards, which incorporate purchased scrapbook supplies as well as the printed card created from digital images, which can be seen in Figures 11.33 and 11.34. Pre-folded card stock can be used for the card, with printed digital images glued to it. Denise has added painted chipboard letters and fabric flowers to complete the cards.

Figure 11.32

Pink Magic kit by Doris Castle, on this book's resource DVD.

Figure 11.33

Greeting card by Denise Doupnik, from the Pink Magic kit.

Figure 11.34

Greeting card by Denise Doupnik, from the Pink Magic kit.

Corinna Stevens also created several hybrid scrapbook projects from Doris's Pink Magic kit. Figure 11.35 shows several cards and mini-albums. A few ribbon scraps, a bit of tulle, paper, and your digital photos and scrapbook components are all that are needed to create these unique paper crafts.

Of course, you can create traditional layouts from this kit, too. Figure 11.36 shows layouts by Michelle Bowley, Corinna Stevens, Donna Gibson, Lizzy Wurmann, Erica Nunez, and Karen Wilhelm, all using the Pink Magic kit in their own way. The kit papers and elements can be combined to create layouts as simple or complex as you like.

Figure 11.35

Greeting cards and mini-albums created by Corinna Stevens, from the Pink Magic kit.

Figure 11.36

Layout variations from the Pink Magic kit.

Sharing Digital the Electronic Way

IT'S NOT ALWAYS FEASIBLE to print your layouts, but you can still share them—the digital way!

Web Galleries

You can display your layouts at many scrapbooking Web forums available on the Internet. These forums require membership (usually free) and will allow you to upload small versions of your layouts, which are then displayed in their user galleries. You should resize your layout to no larger than 600 pixels in its largest dimension for display on the Web (or to e-mail). When in doubt, check with the forum staff for size guidelines before posting your layout in the forum's gallery.

Some Web sites or blog sites allow you to have your own dedicated photo gallery, which you can use to display layouts. Again, don't post full-size layouts; make sure they are small enough to load quickly in an Internet browser.

There are dedicated software applications that can help you create gallery pages with thumbnails (small images that open the larger image when clicked with a mouse cursor). Some freeware gallery creators are

- ⊙ **JAlbum.** Available for download at www.jalbum.net/

- ⊙ **Express Thumbnail Creator.** www.neowise.com

- ⊙ **Lightbox JS Web Gallery Generator.** pranas.net/WebGalleryCreator/

It's not necessary to install additional software if you own Photoshop Elements 5.0 or 6.0. Open the layouts you'd like to show in the gallery in Photoshop Elements. Go to File > Create > Photo Galleries in Elements 5.0. The Organizer will open with the Photo Galleries Wizard, as seen in Figure 11.37, which shows a series of layouts created by Jeannette Mulligan, Novita Solihin, and Lie Fhung, from Fhung's Oh Baby! layout kit on this book's DVD. You can choose a Web Gallery, as well as animated or interactive versions. Choose the template layout and style that you like, and click the Next Step button.

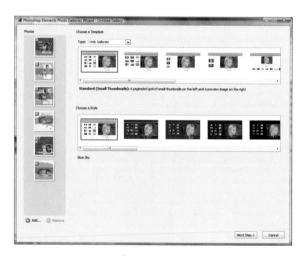

Figure 11.37

Web Gallery creator in Photoshop Elements 5.0.

The next dialog will allow you to create the gallery title and caption and to modify slideshow effects. You can also modify the Web page background, borders, and buttons that will be created. Click the Preview in Browser button to see how your gallery will look when uploaded to a Web site. If you want to modify the template layout or style, click the Previous Step button to return to the preceding dialog.

Figure 11.38

Modify gallery features in the Web Gallery creator of Elements 5.0.

Click the Share button, and the gallery HTML will be created, along with all the necessary files you will need to upload, in the folder you chose. You can upload the entire folder using an FTP application. Some Web sites have their own uploading facility so that you don't need a separate FTP utility. You can also choose to share the Web gallery at Adobe's Photoshop Showcase or share it to CD, as seen in Figure 11.39.

Figure 11.39

Select sharing options in the Web Gallery creator.

Slide Shows on CD or DVD

You can burn a slide show to CD or DVD, as well. Some slide show creator applications are:

- **Picasa.** A versatile editor that can create slide shows and galleries, as well as edit photos, found at picasa.google.com/features/.

- **Slideroll.** Allows you to create Web slide shows and e-mail slide shows as well. www.slideroll.com/

However, you can use Photoshop Elements for this task, too. In Photoshop Elements 6.0, open the layouts you'd like to add to the slide show and click on the Create tab, which will open the Organizer workspace. The Slide Show Preferences dialog, seen in Figure 11.40, will open. You can choose some of the features of the slide show at this point, including background color, transition time, and effects. If you don't want this dialog to pop up each time you create a slide show, uncheck the Show This Dialog Each Time a New Slide Show Is Created box. Click OK.

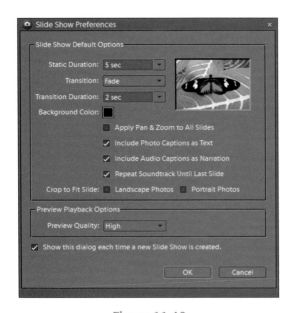

Figure 11.40

Slide show preferences dialog in Photoshop Elements 6.0.

The Slide Show Editor will open, with the layouts you've selected shown in the bottom pane in the order in which they'll be presented in the slide show. You can modify the transitions between each slide, add music or narration, add extra images and text, and blank slides. Figure 11.41 shows the Slide Show Editor panel, with layouts from Lauren Bavin's Blossom Blush kit, which can be found on this book's resource DVD. These layouts have been created by Penny Manning, Tara Drier, Lauren Bavin, and Sally Beacham.

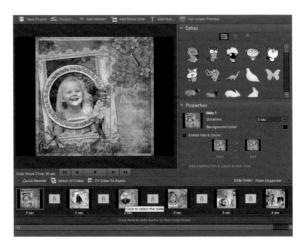

Figure 11.41

Slide Show Editor in Photoshop Elements 6.0.

If you'd like to add text to the slide show, click the Text icon in the Extras palette, or the Add Text menu item at the top of the Editor workspace. Type out the text you'd like, as shown in Figure 11.42. Click OK, and you will be able to re-position the text on the slide.

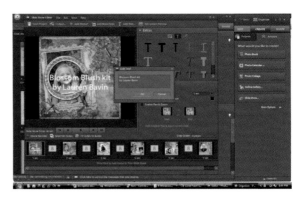

Figure 11.42

Adding text in the Slide Show Editor in Photoshop Elements 6.0.

Once you're satisfied with the slide show, go to File > Output Slide Show, or click the Output menu item at the top of the Slide Show Editor panel. The Slide Show Output dialog, shown in Figure 11.43, will open. This dialog gives you the choice of saving the slide show as a file, burning it to a self-running Video CD that can be viewed on a computer monitor or TV with any DVD player, or creating a Windows Media file. This file can be viewed on a TV screen by using a computer running Windows XP Media Center or Windows Vista.

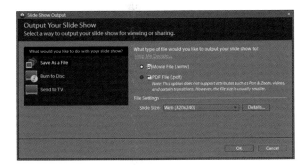

Figure 11.43

Slide Show Output dialog in Photoshop Elements 6.0.

The End and the Beginning

We've reached the end of our book, and now it's time for you to create your own masterpieces. A camera, a computer, and a collection of scrapbooking embellishments are all you need to pass along your memories to your loved ones, for generations to come. Enjoy!

Figure 11.44

"Spice Boy" layout by Sally Beacham,
created from scrapbook components by all our book's designers,
available on the book's resource DVD.

My Favorite Szechuan Dish

Deepfried chicken dice with Szechuan peppers

ADDICTING

I can't never get enough of this truly scrumptious spicy diced chicken from Man Jiang Hong Resto. They have the bestest! I could eat the whole portion on my own. Why! Even 2 portions!

MAN JIANG HONG restaurant in Causeway Bay Feb. 2007

"My Favorite Szechuan Dish" layout by Lie Fhung.

A

Resources

THE RESOURCES LISTED HERE are just the beginning. Be sure to check online search engines for more digital scrapbooking resources. Keep in mind that things on the Web are constantly changing, so some of the links listed may no longer be active.

The Authors' Web Sites

Here are the Web sites of this book's authors, along with two online learning sites where Sally and Lori teach digital scrapbooking classes.

Dizteq by Sally Beacham

www.dizteq.com

Resources, tutorials, tools, and recommendations for Photoshop-compatible plug-in filters. In addition, you'll find some resources for Paint Shop Pro and Xara X, as well as links to great sites.

Lori's Web Graphics by Lori J. Davis

http://loriweb.pair.com

You'll find Web graphics for sure, but also tutorials and goodies for digital scrappers who want to print their creations.

DSU

www.digitalscrapbookplace.com/university/

There are several places online where you can take scrapbook-related courses, and Digital Scrapbook University at Digital Scrapbook Place is one of the best. Lori teaches several classes there, including several on creating components with Paint Shop Pro and one on using graphics tablets.

LVS Online

www.lvsonline.com

LVS Online is another destination for online classes. Lori and Sally developed a class on digital scrapbooking that is offered for self-study there. Sally also has some instructor-led classes in Paint Shop Pro, and Lori has self-study classes on Corel PHOTO-PAINT, Adobe Photoshop Elements, and digital "darkroom" techniques using Paint Shop Pro Photo.

Scrapbooking Magazines

There are many, many scrapbooking magazines, and by the time you read this, there could very well be many more. Check out the Crafts offerings in the periodicals section of your local bookstore or crafts store for the latest in scrapbook magazines. Many magazines have Web sites where you can read articles, access resources, and even submit your work for possible publication. Here are some examples:

Creating Keepsakes

www.creatingkeepsakes.com

Memory Makers

www.memorymakersmagazine.com

Scrapbooks Etc

www.bhgscrapbooksetc.com

Simple Scrapbooks

www.simplescrapbooksmag.com

Digital Scrapbooking Web Sites and Newsgroups

There are dozens of online sites where scrappers can meet, share their ideas, ask questions, and show off their layouts. Here are a few to get you started:

DigiShopTalk

www.digishoptalk.com

Digital Scrapbook Place

www.digitalscrapbookplace.com

Digital Scrapbook Pages

www.digitalscrapbookpages.com

Pages of the Heart

www.pagesoftheheart.net

Scrapbook-Bytes

www.scrapbook-bytes.com

Paint Shop Pro Scrapbook group

news://cnews.corel.com/corel.
PaintShopPro_Scrapbooking

(If you're interested in visiting the Paint Shop Pro Scrapbooking newsgroup, you might first want to go to http://support.corel.com/scripts/rightnow.cfg/php.exe/enduser/std_adp.php?p_faqid=754345 for instructions on how to set up your newsreader and subscribe to the group.)

General Scrapbooking Web Sites

The sites listed here are general scrapping sites, with an emphasis on paper scrapping:

Scrapbook.com

www.scrapbook.com

Scrapbooking.com

www.scrapbooking.com

ScrapbookAddict

www.scrappertalk.com/bbs/

Scrapjazz

www.scrapjazz.com

Scrapbook Designers

There are probably hundreds and hundreds of scrapbook designers active on the Web. Here's information on the designers who contributed sample layouts for the book and kits or templates for the book's DVD.

Lauren Bavin

Lauren Bavin works full time as head designer and instructor for Digital Scrapbook Place (**www.digitalscrapbookplace.com**), heading up a team of 17 designers.

Angela M. Cable

Angela M. Cable (**www.neocognition.com**) is a Web designer, artist, and amateur photographer. Angela has been the technical editor for several publications, including this book.

Doris Castle

Doris Castle, who has a background in graphic design, began delving into digital scrapbooking in 2003. You can track her latest news at her blog and website, **www.DorisCastle.com**.

Roberta D'Achille

Roberta D'Achille's digital scrapping supplies and her Photoshop actions are now carried exclusively at her own store, Rendered Memories (**www.RenderedMemories.com**).

Lie Fhung

Lie Fhung's digital designs are available from several online shops, but her Web site, **Ztampf.com**, is where you can find all of her digital works available to date.

Glenda Ketcham

Glenda Ketcham is a digital designer exclusively at Digital Scrapbook Pages (**www.digitalscrapbook-pages.com**).

Terry Maruca

Terry Maruca is a crafter as well as a digital scrapper. You can find her digital work at **www.scrapbook-elements.com/sbe/** and her traditional craft work in the outlet mall in Lancaster, Pennsylvania.

Image Editor and Photo Album Manufacturers

Serious scrappers need an image editor for creating layouts and maybe even creating their own elements. You don't need to spend US$600 on Adobe Photoshop for high quality. Image editors in the US$100 range are more than adequate. Listed below are the manufacturers of some of the most popular and affordable image editors. These software producers also have other applications that can be useful to the digital scrapper.

Adobe

www.adobe.com

Makers of Photoshop and Photoshop Elements.

Corel

www.corel.com

Makers of Corel Paint Shop Pro Photo, Corel Painter, and the Corel Graphics Suite.

Serif

www.serif.com

Makers of PhotoPlus, DrawPlus, PagePlus, Panorama Plus, and more.

Ulead

www.ulead.com

Makers of PhotoImpact and more. (Ulead is now owned by Corel.)

Digital Camera, Printer, and Scanner Web Sites

Here are a few of the largest and best manufacturers of digital cameras, printers, and scanners:

Canon

www.canon.com

Kodak

www.kodak.com

Epson

www.epson.com

Konica Minolta

www.konicaminolta.com

Fujifilm

www.fujifilm.com

Nikon

www.nikon.com

HP

www.hp.com

Pentax

www.pentax.com

Plug-Ins and Utilities

There are zillions of great plug-ins. Here's just a sampling of sources to get you started. Be warned: plug-in collecting can be quite addictive.

Alien Skin Software

www.alienskin.com

Makers of Eye Candy 5 Impact, Eye Candy 5 Textures, Xenofex 2, Splat!, Snap Art, and more. Alien Skin's Eye Candy and Xenofex plug-in filters are great for creating effects for text, embellishments, and more. Splat! is great for creating borders, edges, frames, and textures. Snap Art is a set of filters for converting photos into digital drawings and paintings. Demos of the Eye Candy filters, Xenofex, Snap Art and Splat! are included on the book's DVD.

AmphiSoft

http://photoshop.msk.ru/as

Makers of several fine freeware and shareware filters. Demos and a few freebies are included on the book's DVD.

Auto FX

www.autofx.com

Makers of many high-quality plug-in filters. Those of particular interest to scrappers are filters in their DreamSuite series and Photo/Graphic Edges. In addition to their commercial filters, they offer a pair of free filter sets: DreamSuite Dreamy Photo and DreamSuite Mosaic.

Autostitch

www.autostitch.net

Autostitch is a free photo stitching program. The same technology that drives the free limited-feature version also drives the more feature-rich versions available commercially, such as Panorama Plus 3 from Serif.

AV Bros.

www.avbros.com

Makers of Page Curl, Puzzle Pro, and Colorist. Page Curl provides two very realistic effects: a turning page effect (Page Curl) and a folding page effect (Page Fold). Puzzle Pro helps you create jigsaw puzzle effects, and it also produces various other high-quality image effects. Colorist is a small, handy stand-alone program that lets you choose a color, and then get its RGB, HSB, and Hex values using the program's color wheel or a large library of named colors. Demos of each of these are included on the book's DVD.

ColorSchemer

www.colorschemer.com

ColorSchemer is an easy-to-use color matching application that will help you select creative color schemes. A demo is included on the book's DVD.

namesuppressed

www.namesuppressed.com

Tone your digital photos, create plaid patterns, and add dreamy effects with the shareware plug-in filters from namesuppressed: Autochromatic, Plaid Lite, and Softener (demos are included on the book's DVD). Many scrappers are particularly fond of Plaid Lite, which takes colors from an image and uses those colors to create beautiful plaid patterns.

Redfield Plugins

www.redfieldplugins.com

You can find many wonderful plug-ins—some free and some at a modest price—at Redfield Plugins. Redfield's plug-ins are great for creating texturing and similar effects. A nice sampling is included on the book's DVD.

The Plugin Site

www.thepluginsite.com

Harry Heim's The Plugin Site is a great place for information on plug-ins and for lots and lots of great filters, both by Harry and others. Among Harry's fine filters and utilities are ColorWasher and FocalBlade (for photo correction and enhancement), PhotoFreebies (a set of free filters for photo manipulation), Edge and Frame Galaxy (a great utility for adding decorative edges and colored frames to images), and the recently released Plugin Galaxy 2 (a collection of lots of nifty special effect and toning filters). PhotoFreebies and demos of several of Harry's commercial plug-ins and utilities are included on the book's DVD.

TwistingPixels

www.twistingpixels.com

Makers of ArtStudioPro Volumes 1 and 2, PixelCreation, PixelPaper, PixelPack, and PixelSampler. The ArtStudioPro suites are collections of photographic filters, while the other suites offer collections of special effects filters that will be of interest to scrappers. Demos of all the TwistingPixels filter packages are included on the book's DVD.

Fonts

Every scrapbooker needs at least a few more fonts than what you'll find as standards on your operating system. Here's a sampling of sources for free and commercial fonts. Search online, and you'll find many more.

Astigmatic One Eye Typographic Institute

www.astigmatic.com

Designers of a large collection of gorgeous commercial and free fonts.

House of Lime

www.houseoflime.com

Source of many fine fonts and dingbats, some specifically designed with scrappers in mind.

King Things

http://mysite.wanadoo-members.co.uk/ Kingthings/index.htm

Kevin King is an artist and photographer as well as a font designer. He has some wonderful fonts, including many decorated fonts. Samples are included on the book's DVD.

Larabie Fonts and Typodermic

www.larabiefonts.com   www.typodermic.com

Ray Larabie's fonts are some of the best around. Check out his extensive collections of free fonts at Larabie Fonts and his commercial fonts at Typodermic. Samples are included on the book's DVD.

The Dingbat Pages

www.dingbatpages.com

Extensive compendium of dingbat fonts from a variety of designers. Fonts are available as freeware, shareware, guiltware, charityware, and postcardware.

Typadelic Fonts

www.typadelic.com

Beautiful fonts—from grungy to lovely—from font designer Ronna Penner.

Scrapbook-Bytes

www.scrapbook-bytes.com

Many scrapbook sites also offer fonts. Among these is Scrapbook-Bytes, and two of their font designers—Melissa Baxter and Miss Tiina—contributed fonts for inclusion on this book's DVD.

Clip Art

Clip art is ready-made line art and photos that you can use in your designs. You probably have some already bundled with your word processor, office suite, image editor, or other applications. Here's one of the most popular commercial sources.

Dover

www.doverpublications.com

Dover Publications offers numerous clip art collections, many of them of particular interest to scrappers. Be sure to sign up to receive their weekly free samplers.

Online Photo Sharing and Printing

There are many excellent sites where you can share your photos with others, order prints, and maybe even create a hardcover book of your photos or layouts. Here are a few examples:

Ofoto

www.ofoto.com

Shutterfly

www.shutterfly.com

Snapfish

www.snapfish.com

Another service that offers hardcover binding of layouts is Bound 2 Remember **(www.bound2remember.com).**

Web Hosts

If you'd like to have your own Web site without spending a lot of money, here are a couple places to check out:

Angelfire

www.angelfire.com

Tripod

www.tripod.com

To find other possibilities, go to any online search engine and type in "web host."

General Photography and Scanning-Related Web Sites

Chances are that if you're a scrapper, you're also an amateur photographer (or maybe even a pro). To learn more about photography and scanning, begin with these helpful sites.

Digital Photography Review

www.dpreview.com

Plenty of reviews of cameras and related hardware along with informative articles, instructional material, and much more.

Scan Tips

www.scantips.com

Wayne Fulton's classic fact-filled site on, you guessed it, tips about scanning.

Paper Suppliers

If you print out your layouts, you'll need paper. Printer manufacturers offer papers specifically designed for their particular printers. In addition, you can find high-quality papers at specialty paper suppliers, such as the ones listed below.

Hawk Mountain Papers

www.hawkmtpaper.com

Family owned and operated, Hawk Mountain supplies premium inkjet papers for photographic and fine art printing.

Strathmore Artist Papers

www.strathmoreartist.com

Strathmore has been manufacturing fine art papers since 1899. Today they continue to supply high-quality papers, including fine art and photographic inkjet papers. In addition, they have kits for greeting cards, calendars, and photo albums.

Index

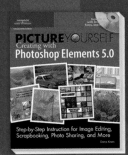

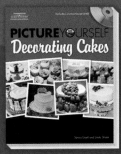

License Agreement/Notice of Limited Warranty